Love
IS A
Flame

L o v

FOREWORD BY

GARY CHAPMAN

Compiled by JAMES STUART BELL

e is a

Flame

BETHANY HOUSE PUBLISHERS

Minneapolis, Minnesota

Published by Bethany House Publishers
11400 Hampshire Avenue South
Bloomington, Minnesota 55438

Bethany House Publishers is a division of
Baker Publishing Group, Grand Rapids, Michigan.

Printed in the United States of America

Library of Congress Cataloging-in-Publication Data

Love is a flame : stories of what happens when love is rekindled / compiled by James Stuart Bell ; foreword by Gary Chapman.
    p. cm.
    Summary: "A compilation of inspiring true stories of enduring married love"—Provided by publisher.
    ISBN 978-0-7642-0807-2 (pbk. : alk. paper) 1. Marriage. 2. Love. 3. Married people. I. Bell, James S.
    HQ734.L758   2010
    248.8'44—dc22

2010006248

Dedicated to my wife,

Margaret,

who has kept the flame burning
for thirty-three years.

ACKNOWLEDGMENTS

Credit goes to my chief editor, Kyle Duncan, who had the same vision to extend the *Love Is a Verb* concept to marriages; to Julie Smith and Ellen Chalifoux for superb editorial assistance; and to my friend Tim Peterson for his creative and enthusiastic marketing efforts.

James Stuart Bell

CONTENTS

FOREWORD

Marriage is a journey through unchartered waters. When we made those huge promises of "for better or for worse," we never truly expected it to get worse. "For richer or for poorer" seemed unrealistic. How could we ever get poorer? Of course, we knew that "in sickness and in health" were both realities, but sickness comes at the end of life. In short, none of us were prepared for the real world of living in covenant with a spouse who is more human than divine.

The old saying is "Truth is stranger than fiction." I would add, "And it's much more powerful." Real stories, written by real people, in their own words; that is what you'll find in *Love Is a Flame*. As I read these stories I found myself laughing, crying, and reflecting on my own marriage and the hundreds of couples who have walked in and out of my counseling office over the past thirty years.

I do not mean to imply that these are stories of couples who have found healing via counseling. For the most part the authors never entered a counselor's office. But the lives they have experienced, and the conclusions they have drawn, remind me of the pain and the joy that most of us have experienced. The insights that James Bell gives at the conclusion of each story shed the kind of light every counselor seeks to bring to his clients.

As you read these stories, you will remember the ups and downs of your own marriage, and you will also observe the patterns of life you have seen in the marriages of your friends. I hope you will be grateful as you reflect on the lessons you have learned, and I hope you will be open to try some of the ideas that have brought success to other marriages. Learning from the failures and successes of others is much cheaper than going to see a counselor. So laugh, cry, and learn as you read *Love Is a Flame: Stories of What Happens When Love Is Rekindled.*

—GARY CHAPMAN, PhD, AUTHOR OF
THE FIVE LOVE LANGUAGES

There it is.
Just a spark.
It flickers.
It glows.
It grows.
As it increases, it brings light to the darkest corners.
It brings warmth and life to the coldest hearts.
Love is a flame that sets our world aglow.
Love, like fire, is one of the most powerful forces on earth; one of
God's greatest gifts.
And marriage is a hearth in which it flourishes.
In these pages, you'll see different nuances of that love flame.
You'll see the people who stoke that flame to bring even more warmth
and light into their marriage through prayer, acceptance,
kindness, and practical actions.
You'll meet those who learn how to fan the flames into the fire of
passion that only two can share.
You'll see the flame roar to life, to vanquish the darkness of
confusion, fear, and misunderstanding.
You'll see how in other marriages the flame of love rises up to purify
and burn out the dross and ills that threaten a relationship–
pornography, adultery, and even apathy.
And you'll even see the embers of forgiveness and tenderness bring
reassurance and comfort during the glowing moments of life.
So come. Sit back and put another log on the fire.
See how you, too, can make the flames dance steadier, brighter in the
hearth of your marriage.

–James Stuart Bell

We'll Always Have Paris

They call it the seven-year itch. That's the dangerous season many marriages enter after the thrill of newlywed bliss has faded and the reality of bills, kids, and busyness has knocked most of the romance from the relationship. Mine was more like a seventeen-year itch.

My husband, Rob, and I met during college through InterVarsity Christian Fellowship. After spending a week together at a leadership training seminar, Rob asked me if I'd ever considered being a pastor's wife.

Whoa, boy! I thought. *I've only known you seven days.*

But we had an unmistakably close connection and a common commitment to ministry. In spite of two more academic years on separate campuses and summers separated by a whole ocean, we watched God confirm our call to each other.

We married soon after graduation. I sailed out of the church on the arm of my groom, sure that the years to come would be marked by idyllic moments of wedded delight and romantic trysts.

But our honeymoon was cut short by illness, and like most couples, our first year was full of adjusting to the practical aspects of living together—without driving each other nuts.

Rob fell in love with my joyful impulsiveness and *joie de vivre*, but found my chronic lateness and disorganization less endearing. And the calm solidity that first attracted me to Rob had begun to seem dull and unimaginative. Where was the fun, spontaneous romance of our courtship?

By year seventeen of our marriage, we had come pretty far. Five years after we married, Rob finished seminary. I taught high school English. We led youth groups, started a church, and tried to start a family.

But life proved a lot more challenging than I had dreamed the day we said "I do." Rob and I learned how to put wheels on our promises to stick by one another in "sickness and health," "for better or worse," "for richer or poorer." We weathered serious illness, infertility, miscarriages, financial stressors, multiple moves and jobs, two children, and the joys and rigors of ministry life.

Year seventeen found us serving in our second pastorate, a tiny church on Cape Cod. We had two adorable kids but too many bills, so Rob painted houses to supplement our income. If anyone had asked me at the time, I believe I would have said that we were happy and that life was good. But my fortieth birthday was approaching and life didn't look as glossy or glamorous as I had imagined it would be. Though I appeared all right on the surface, underneath I was a little numb, a little disappointed, and more than a little tired of the sameness and struggle of each day!

One morning after the kids boarded the school bus, Rob told me to sit down. He had something to tell me.

Oh, this won't be good, I thought, steeling myself for the blow.

"I know your fortieth birthday is coming, and I really wanted to surprise you," Rob began.

Hmmm . . . maybe this isn't cataclysmic after all, I mused.

"But I can't forge your passport signature," he continued.

Did I hear the word passport?

"So I'll need you to sign here, because I'm taking you to Paris for your birthday."

I was glad Rob had told me to sit down, because I just about fell on the floor. Since I'd studied French, traveling to Paris with my husband was right at the top of my "bucket list."

Two months later Rob and I were winging our way across the Atlantic, ready for a trip made possible by his careful saving from extra painting jobs God provided. After checking into our hotel, we took our first *promenade* into the city. Hopping onto the Metro, we headed for Sacré Coeur.

From the top of the hill where the lovely white cathedral rests, we could see over the city below, including the Eiffel Tower in the distance. We enjoyed *bifteck* and *pommes frites* at a small restaurant in Montmartre, drinking in the atmosphere and each other's company. Later that night Rob hired an artist to draw my portrait. I sat there while she put the finishing touches on the picture, the strains of "La Vie en Rose" wafting across the heart of Montmartre. Rob and I walked hand in hand through the City of Lights, not Pastor and Mrs. Rienstra, not Daddy and Mommy, just Rob and Lynne.

The next day we explored the Left Bank and later found Rob's favorite Dutch masters at the Louvre. Together we discovered the wonder of the Musée d'Orsay and reveled in the beauty of impressionist works that come alive in its light-filled galleries.

As we walked the streets and galleries of Paris, Rob and I started to rewind to a place in our relationship we hadn't visited in years. We missed our two children and wondered how they were, but we also talked about the art we were seeing and what it meant to us. We discussed ideas. We dreamed. We simply enjoyed one another.

The night of my fortieth birthday, we took out the crystal flutes from our wedding toast that I had stashed in my satchel. In broken French, I convinced the security guard at the Eiffel Tower to let us make a toast on the top observation deck. There, the city shimmering beneath us, we toasted my birthday, one another, and our love.

Our last evening in Paris, Rob and I wandered by the Seine. Nearby floated several *bateaux mouches*, the glass-enclosed boats that glide under the countless bridges of Paris. We decided to take in the glittering city from the top of the boat, apart from the other passengers. From there, we could reach up and touch the bottoms of the bridges as we passed under them.

I don't remember whether it was as we passed under the *Pont Neuf* or the *Pont Alexandre*. All I know is that somewhere on that boat ride, we found our way back to each other's hearts. The cool April night meant we had to snuggle to stay warm atop the open-air boat, and later that night . . . well, as the French put it, *ooh la la.*

Was it the change of setting, the gift of uninterrupted time together, or the magic of Paris? Did it happen on the top of the Eiffel Tower or as we wandered the back streets of the Latin Quarter? Somewhere amid the beauty of a foreign city, Rob and I recaptured our romance, a gift from the heart of our loving God.

Even now, when the bills begin to mount, the needs of others weigh heavy, and we begin to lose touch with one another, my sweet, solid husband takes me in his arms, kisses me, and reminds me, "We'll always have Paris, Schweetheart."

Bogey would be proud.

—LYNNE RIENSTRA

⌒

Maybe you can't take a trip to Paris—unless it's Paris, Missouri; or Paris, Illinois; or one of the other dozens of cities named Paris in North America. However, every marriage needs those special trips, adventures, or events that are memorable. We all need evenings, weekends, and even weeks away from the distractions of everyday life. Those sometimes-stolen moments allow us to focus on each other as the real world fades into a hazy distance. Then, when we're back in the cold, harsh realities of normal living, memories of those special times give us a glimpse of light and hope when the marriage flames seem to flicker low. As we have those "Here's looking at you, kid" occasions, they remind us of the beginning—and the continuation—of a beautiful relationship.

While He Was Sleeping

They say you can't change your marriage overnight, but one all-nighter changed everything for us.

It was our first year of marriage and I was lying in bed, glaring at my husband, who was sleeping soundly on our hand-me-down mattress that tilted slightly to one side.

How can you sleep when you know that I am furious with you?

I seethed so hard that he should have felt my hot, hateful breath on his neck. After my huffing and puffing did not wake him, I threw off the covers and stomped into the living room, waiting for him to come looking for me.

Finally I realized he wasn't coming.

He doesn't care. I fumed. *Too selfish to miss his precious sleep just to save our marriage!*

My emotions escalated as I looked at our wedding picture on the wall.

"I hate him!" I said it and I meant it. I hated him for lying so comfortably in there while I was so uncomfortably upset out here. I finally fell onto the couch in a heap of endless sobs.

After my tears subsided, I turned on the television and stared hopelessly at the tube, mindlessly watching infomercials. I had cried too many tears to care anymore, so now I just sat. I was trapped and I had to live out my fate with an uncaring husband.

But as the hours ticked by, I started wondering, *How did I get here?*

Clay most certainly tricked me into marrying him. Before we were married, he played the part of the adoring boyfriend, surprising me with extravagant dates, scavenger hunts, and poetry. And what did he do as soon as I was legally bound to him for life? He warped into a lazy, football-watching, eye-rolling lump on the couch.

This is not what I signed up for, I thought. I felt like a contestant on one of those hidden-camera TV shows, only this episode would last forever—until death did we part.

After a few hours of flipping channels and gritting my teeth, it dawned on me. *Maybe Clay doesn't know that I'm miserable. Maybe he honestly believes that everything is fine, that we just had a little squabble. That is why he is able to sleep like a baby while I'm so unhappy. I just need to tell him how I feel and explain exactly what I need from him.*

I got up and made a pot of coffee. It didn't matter that it was two o'clock in the morning; I needed to fortify myself to do the most important work of my life—save my marriage.

As the coffeepot perked, I grabbed the closest pen and my trusty journal and feverishly began to write. I felt divinely inspired to clearly articulate my innermost desires. I envisioned the perfect spouse, compared him to Clay, and reported the deficit in my notebook.

After filling four pages, I took a deep breath and propped my feet on the ottoman. It was too late to go to bed now. I just sat there rereading my inspired revelations. I revised it and finished. The work was good, all neatly printed in black and white—a bulleted list of necessary needs.

I felt pleased. I had figured it all out, and in a generous moment I decided to make my husband breakfast. My moment of satisfaction was followed by immediate panic. *How is Clay going to react to this list?*

It was a long list. I was afraid he would be overwhelmed. This might be too much for a Saturday morning. *He will probably enjoy the eggs I'm cooking but resent the side order of sizzling criticism.*

I decided to shorten the list, to choose just the most important needs. Carefully rereading the list again, I circled only what was absolutely necessary.

Number one: unconditional love. That was a keeper. So I circled it.

Number two: lots of encouragement. I need that every day. Doesn't everyone? I couldn't scratch number two. So I circled it.

Number three: complete understanding of my feelings. Of course, I circled it.

Number four: willingness to listen to all of my ideas. *Oh, he won't even be listening by this time.* I circled it anyway.

And the list went on and on. How could I possibly choose which of my needs were most important? *I need it all!* I flipped through the pages one more time, and a crazy thought came to my mind.

What if Clay can't give me everything I need?

It wasn't a sad thought. It was a moment of clarity. The coffee, chocolate, Cheetos, and sleep deprivation swirled together to create a flash of insight: *What if my husband can't be my all in all?*

I examined the list with that idea in mind. I wanted someone to unconditionally love me, accept me, praise me, encourage me, listen to me, and on and on. Clay would have to quit his job, forget all his friends, and study my every move in order to fulfill all my wishes. It was utterly impossible for him to be the person I described in my journal.

Suddenly I felt sorry for the poor man who married me. At this rate, he would never be able to live up to my endless expectations. I pictured our life years later, with him as a frustrated, middle-aged man, weary from his wife's unrealistic demands on his time and attention.

I rarely talk to myself out loud, but that morning as the sun shone on empty junk-food wrappers, I uttered five words that have forever changed our marriage: "He is just a man."

He is not my God. He is not my mom. He is not my doctor, therapist, or gal pal. "He is just a man." He will not heal my wounds or solve my problems. He did not stand at the altar on our wedding day and promise to be my Alpha and Omega. He promised to love me in good times and bad, in sickness and health, for richer or poorer. And I promised him the same.

One night.

Two cups of coffee.

Four pages in my journal.

A beautiful sunrise.

A new day with a man I love. He is just a man—the man I love.

—EMILY OSBURNE

*M*ost of us would never think we believe in superheroes. Yet, in essence, we expect the one we married to be Superspouse. No matter how our culture has changed, men tend to expect their wives to work, take care of the kids, keep the house clean, and be the ideal, romantic wife. And women tend to expect men to work, take time with the kids, help clean the house, and then be the ideal, romantic husband.

When something seems amiss in our marriages, maybe the first thing we should do is look at our expectations. Superspouse doesn't exist any more than Superman, Batman, or Spiderman does. When, as Emily noted, we realize that only God can meet all the emotional needs in our lives, and we comprehend that we live with a fallible human, it takes the pressure off of a spouse—and off of a marriage, too!

Moonlight, Roses, and Kids With Stuffed Noses

How about going to bed early tonight?" my husband whispers in my ear.

I rinse the last supper dish and ask coyly, "What do you have in mind?"

"I want to carry you to bed and have my way with you," he says in a darn good Harrison Ford impersonation.

"I'll meet you in the bedroom."

With a wink of the eye and a wiggle of the hips, I saunter out of the kitchen. The seductive ploy is sadly spoiled when I smash my toe on the doorjamb and grunt in pain. Kate Capshaw helped Harrison Ford escape a doomed temple or something; I can barely make it out of my own kitchen.

I hustle the kids through homework and baths.

"Skip math tonight; that's what computers are for. No, you don't need soap; just a quick rinse will do. I read somewhere that a little dirt is good for your skin; it protects you from ultraviolet rays," I advise.

"Pick out a bedtime story, a short one. *Bambi*? How about a condensed version: Bambi lives, his mother doesn't, he wins the fight, they all live happily ever after. Except for his mother. No, I don't know why a deer is king of the forest if a lion is king of the jungle. Yes, Bambi's a boy even though he has a girl's name.

"Let's say our prayers. There we go. Into bed. Hug, hug, kiss, kiss. I love you, too. And you. And you. And you. Good night. Good night. Good night. Good night."

I'm glad I have only four kids, I think.

Finally the kids are tucked away and the lights are out. I head toward the *boudoir*, where I slip into something slinky. At least, it *used* to slink. Now it kind of . . . snugs.

Oh well. I brush my teeth and comb my hair, dab my best perfume behind my ears, turn off the lamp, and light some candles. With the comforter turned down invitingly, I arrange myself in a glamorous pose among the pillows. I ignore the Snoopy pillowcase beside me; my bed linens have not matched since the Reagan era.

The door opens. In a throaty voice I say, "I've been waiting for you, big boy."

"I can't sleep," a tiny voice whimpers.

Whoops.

"What's wrong, honey?" I ask as I scramble into my robe.

"My tummy hurts. And my head. Can I sleep in your room?"

"No." I take Michael's little hand and lead him back to bed.

"You smell good, Mommy."

"Thank you." I tuck the covers securely. Would it be child abuse to nail the blankets down so they sort of immobilize him? Only temporarily, of course.

"Why are there candles in your room, Mommy?"

"Because she and Daddy want to smooch, that's why," says Josh, with all the worldly wisdom of a twelve-year-old boy.

"Good *night*." More hugs, more kisses.

Back in my bedroom, I shrug off the robe and climb back into bed. I settle against the pillows just as a yawn splits open my skull. "Those kids better go to sleep and Rick better come to bed *fast*," I mutter.

"Mo-o-om," someone calls.

"*What?*" I bellow. Did Kate bellow at Harrison?

"Josh's arm is hanging down."

I grab my robe and stomp to the boys' room.

"What's wrong with his arm hanging down?" I demand.

"It's bugging me," says Jason.

I glare at Josh, who is lying calmly on his stomach in the top bunk with his arm dangling over. "Why is your arm hanging down?"

"I want it to," he says.

"Well, *don't*." I turn to leave.

"Mommy, I still can't sleep," Michael whines.

"Close your eyes. It helps."

Back to the bedroom. The candles are flickering low; Snoopy has landed on the floor. I toss my robe somewhere and crawl beneath the covers. Forget glamour. And boy does this negligee *itch*. Good grief. How did the pioneers manage to have so many kids when they all slept together in one room?

"Mommy, I'm sick."

I roll out of bed, find my robe, and turn to see Michael standing in the doorway again. Wordlessly I take him into the bathroom.

"Let's get you a drink of water." I sigh. "Maybe that will help."

When I turn on the light, I see how flushed his cheeks are. He feels feverish, and his nose is so stuffy he can hardly breathe. Instantly I change from Kate Capshaw to Florence Nightingale.

"Poor baby," I murmur. I give him medicine and a drink of water, and once again tuck him snugly into bed. I caress his cheek and say, "Call me if you need me, baby; I'm right there in the next room."

Once more, I head back to the bedroom.

I hear Rick's snores before I even reach the door; he must have come to bed and fallen asleep while I was with Michael.

I blow out the candles and change into a warm flannel nightgown. In the dark, I manage to find Snoopy and drop wearily into bed.

"I guess we're just not meant to be Harrison Ford and Kate Capshaw," I whisper, dropping a kiss on Rick's shoulder.

Without waking up, Rick turns over and cuddles me close to him. I yawn and then drift to sleep with his arms around me.

Eat your heart out, Ms. Capshaw.

—RHONDA WHEELER STOCK

Sometimes even the best-planned or most-hoped-for romantic interludes are just doomed not to happen. The joy of marriage is that we can enjoy the companionship and the give-and-take of romance without the pressure to perform. We don't always have to impress with death-defying stunts in the bedroom to enjoy the adventure of togetherness. Instead, we can appreciate the comfortable security of having a loving spouse who won't get bent out of shape if demands of real life intrude and postpone those longed-for intimate rendezvous. And that's a cache that surpasses anything the greatest treasure hunter could hope for!

Encouraging My Dream

The serendipity overwhelmed me.

I stood in a conference room at the Marriott-Burkshire Hotel in Towson, Maryland, surrounded by people who shared my love of writing and authors whose work I'd cherished for years. Here *they* were, mingling with us, informally sharing their experiences as if we were equals.

I'd taken a huge step by submitting my fiction to this prestigious "writing boot camp." Beyond all my expectations, I'd been accepted. I was to spend an entire weekend cloistered with master storytellers learning to work on my heart's desire: learning to tell a great story.

The event's importance ran second only to getting married and having children. I'm a simple person. Always have been. All I've ever wanted from life is a family and a writing career. So that Friday night felt like destiny unfolding.

After several opening panels during which I'd scribbled pages of notes, my head swirled. Around midnight, however, the adrenaline faded and I felt the fatigue of the earlier five-hour drive. Knowing that Saturday would be a busy day, I decided to get some sleep. I wanted to be completely focused on this dream I was living, and I didn't want anything to interfere.

I retired to my hotel room and called home to say good-night to my wife. After several rings, though, everything changed.

"H-hello?"

My wife, Abby's, voice sounded high and shrill. Static crackled as she apparently jostled the phone between her cheek and shoulder. That meant her hands weren't free.

I shivered. *Why aren't her hands free at this time of night?* Then I heard a sound that probably every young parent recognizes—the shallow rasps of croup.

"Madi's sick. Zack's sick, too. He's sleeping. I'm taking Madi outside, but it's *so* cold! I don't know what to do. . . ."

My youngest child, Zack, had suffered from croup all week. It was Zack's third or fourth time to have croup that season. Abby and I had gotten little sleep the night before. I'd driven to Maryland after only three hours of rest. Friday morning I'd debated not going to the conference at all.

As usual, my wife was the epitome of logic. "Honey, we've already rented the car for you. You need this. You applied for this conference on the last day of registration and they immediately accepted you. That *means* something. You have to go."

When I left at noon, Zack sounded better, and Madi had developed what seemed to be a simple cold. Going seemed right. Safe, even.

That night, separated from my wife and sick children by five hours and hundreds of miles, nothing felt safe. I felt helpless as I heard my wife fumbling to get Madi ready to go outside into the biting January cold.

We knew of two basic home remedies for croup: shower steam to ease throat irritation and cold air to bring down throat swelling.

If Abby was taking Madi outside on such a cold night, the steam hadn't worked, which meant things were bad.

Once outside, my wife said, "Talk to Madi. She's scared."

The phone rattled as Abby passed it to my daughter. "D-daddy? It h-hurts. It hurts!"

It's one thing to hear a toddler cry, another thing to listen to a four-year-old girl rasp—she's old enough to know she can't breathe, but not old enough to know why. Her voice trembled, cracking at the edges. Each breath sounded sharp and short, as if her lung capacity were quartered. Fear hammered me.

I can't remember what futile words of comfort I offered. Then my wife took back the phone and I said, "Listen. I'm coming home. The highways will be empty; I can be there by four or five."

In a slightly trembling but firmer voice, Abby said, "*No*. That makes no sense. We'll be okay. I just need to get her settled so I can get upstairs before Zack starts coughing."

A deep sense of shame pervaded me.

How selfish I am. My wife is alone with two young children who are very sick. This is not as important as they are. I should be there. I should go home.

"This *isn't* that important. I can leave, be home in—"

"No!" A pause. "This *is* important. For you. For us. You *need* to stay there. I'll be fine. Madi's better already. You *can't* come home."

Very rarely does my wife put her foot down, but when she does, it's firm, and it had just been put down in defense of something I'd dreamed of for years. As I hung up the phone, I knew that no matter what I achieved on paper, nothing could ever overshadow the love my wife was showing.

I called Abby's mother, who lived roughly fifteen minutes away from us, and asked for *her* opinion, looking for a maternal authority to quiet the guilt nipping my heels. She agreed it made better sense for me not to rush home, that aid would be close should things get worse. This helped.

As I drifted into an uneasy sleep, I thought about how thankful I was for my wife.

Being married to a writer isn't easy. I'm not sure *I'd* be up to it. It all sounds so romantic and exciting when an eager, clueless fellow courts his intended and regales her with dreams of his writing career. Soon enough, however, the supporting spouse faces the harsh realities of living with a writer: the writer-spouse isolating him or herself for hours while the other half is left to tend to home, hearth, and children who may be part Tasmanian devil.

And of course, initial success is minimal, often bolstering self-esteem but not the family budget. Years pass and rejections pile up while the writer sinks ever more deeply into his or her little writing world. The spouse understandably begins to ask, "How much longer until you reach the success you promised? When will we actually start making money? Or at least enough to pay the baby-sitter while you spend summer days writing instead of watching the kids?"

A vast chasm lies between a writer's dreams and the realities of a writing career. That night, Abby could have easily said, "Enough. Time for you to stop playing writer and come home. I need you!"

But she didn't. She did something I think very few spouses do today: she believed in me. She believed in something she didn't understand, a goal she didn't share. She put her full weight behind a dream that wasn't hers.

The next day I sat in workshops with bestselling novelists and was able to pick their brains at mixers. I learned they were humans with the same hopes, dreams, and fears as I had.

I called Abby several times Saturday. Madi's croup had faded, and though Zack's cough had flared up, offering my wife little rest, they'd survived. Abby sounded tired yet seemed happy I didn't have to come home.

Any parent who has battled croup knows that while it fades with sunlight, it strikes back at night . . . and evening was approaching.

Later, after more panels and workshops, I took a deep breath, said a prayer, and called home. Abby's voice lacked the panic of the night before, but its weariness pulled at my guts. In the background I heard thin, telltale rasps.

"Oh *no*. Again? I thought they were better."

"They were. But then Zack started coughing and vomiting." She sighed. "It's not as bad as last night, but we're in for a long haul, I think."

"Listen. Most things are done here," I stated. "I met some great people and learned a lot. I'll come home."

"No. You're supposed to stay," she countered. "We'll be fine. You need to finish this."

I was confused. I'd experienced and learned much. Sunday's events would mostly be formalities. I had no reason or need to stay, except . . .

One thing. I hadn't told Abby for fear of influencing her. But a few hours earlier, I'd received a returned copy of a story that had been critiqued by an editor. He'd written a note suggesting that I talk to him about it on Sunday.

Again, Abby wouldn't hear of my leaving. I stayed. The next day I met with a man who has since become a mentor for me. And he gave me my first professional writing assignment.

I was realizing my dreams—and all because my wife believed in me. She had faith in the gifts God gave me. She supported my pursuit of something that doesn't interest her at all. And she encouraged my dreams, which often make our situation in life more complicated than it otherwise would be.

That kind of belief is one of the highest expressions of love.

–KEVIN LUCIA

⌒

We don't have to be the artistic type of person to have dreams. God built into each of our lives a little bit of His ability and desire to create. And He gives each of us a unique blend of His gifts and abilities.

One of the best ways we can truly know another person is to learn and understand those desires and gifts God has given him or her. Often, in the daily busyness of life, we lose sight of that side of our spouse. Sometimes it takes effort to look for a beloved's secret aspirations. And dreams are fragile. They must be nurtured. Sometimes a person feels it's foolish or selfish to spend the time and energy to pursue dreams. That's where a loving spouse, like Abby, can step in. We can give our loved one support, understanding, and encouragement—even a kind of permission—to explore aspirations. Often it takes sacrifice on our part. But when we believe in the one we love, it gives him or her wings to fly to new heights.

True Confessions

I guess there never is a good time for your world to fall apart, but this was a particularly bad day. My husband, Jeff, and I were scrambling as we prepared for his parents' arrival from Texas. Jeff, a pastor of a small inner-city church, had been burning the candle at both ends preparing for a community ministry project. As church planters, we never seemed to have enough hours in the day to get everything done.

When Jeff got home from work, I asked him how his meeting that morning had gone. He was evasive and I could tell immediately that something was wrong.

Jeff explained that he had once again fallen into pornography. But this time was different; he'd gotten caught. Our denominational leaders had confronted him that morning, knowing he had watched Internet pornography while in the office.

Not only was my husband told to step down from his pastorate, but the leaders also wanted us to leave the area quickly. My mind raced as I tried to absorb it all.

We had been church planters in Buffalo, New York, for almost seven years. Most of our friends and family thought we were crazy for leaving the South after graduating from seminary, but it was a dream come true to raise our family and serve the Lord in this close-knit, blue-collar community. I had told many people that I could see us living in Buffalo the rest of our lives.

The loss of our ministry hurt most as I cried in Jeff's arms. I let him console me, but inside, my anger grew. My husband's selfishness and lack of self-control had just ruined my life. How could he do this to our family? What were we going to do?

Early in our marriage, Jeff had confessed to me that he struggled with Internet pornography. I was surprised. When I had met Jeff in seminary, I was drawn to him because of his spiritual maturity and discipline. He loved preaching and teaching God's Word. Pornography seemed completely out of character. Because he had come to me, I believed him when he said he was ready to rid his life of pornography. I offered to help in any way I could.

While he enjoyed a period of victory, it was later followed by another confession and a promise to try harder. After the third confession, I told him I was not going to live in fear that he was going to get caught and be one more fallen preacher to embarrass the church. I asked him to meet with a Christian counselor and find out if he needed to step out of ministry.

The counselor felt Jeff could continue to serve in ministry while working on his problem. We put filters on our computer and Jeff set up an accountability relationship with another pastor. In the following months, Jeff assured me that pornography was no longer a stumbling block, and I believed him.

In reality, Jeff found ways around the computer filter, his accountability partner fell through, and he lied to me for months to keep the charade going. His use of porn had grown deeper and darker and he felt powerless to give it up. And now, the game was over.

As I stood with him in the kitchen, I realized that Jeff was completely broken. For years he had convinced himself that using pornography wasn't a big deal. Now it had cost him his ministry, his home, and perhaps his family. He was overwhelmed with guilt, shame, and fear. I had never seen him so lost. Everything around us was falling apart. Clearly, someone needed to be stable.

I've always been able to switch off my emotions fairly easily, so I responded to the challenge by kicking into survival mode. It would be almost an entire year before I dealt with my sadness and anger in a healthy way, but for now, we had so many major decisions to make. Our denominational leaders wanted us to move. Should we? If so, where? Would we be able to sell our home? How long would it take for us to find new jobs?

At that point, I took over the reins of our marriage. I told Jeff I would not leave him. While we both questioned whether moving was necessary, we decided to trust our leaders' wisdom. I decided we should move to North Carolina to be closer to my family.

By the end of the night, we had come up with a basic plan of action. I still felt as if my world was spinning out of control, but at least we had a sense of direction.

We stumbled through the rest of the week, telling just a handful of people what was happening. Jeff told his parents the full story while they were visiting. I called a dear friend and asked her to pray. Despite their words of encouragement, we still felt incredibly alone. Jeff was on the brink of depression as we packed boxes and prepared our house to sell.

The most difficult confession was yet to come. While our denominational leaders suggested we not tell our church family what was going on, we felt we couldn't just leave without an explanation. We decided to tell the church leaders privately after church on Sunday. I held back tears during the entire service, knowing we were about to turn our church family upside down. Jeff's voice broke as he confessed to our leaders and apologized to each of them for letting them down. They were loving, supportive, and forgiving.

We decided to tell the rest of the church family that our marriage was in trouble and we would be stepping down from ministry to work on reconciliation. Jeff delivered the news during our weekly Bible study. People were shocked, but they still expressed love for our family. Our final worship service with that sweet church felt like a funeral service to me.

While Jeff and I waited for our house to sell and the next chapter to unfold, we attended a large church in a nearby community. Nobody there knew us, or our secret. Although other Christians surrounded us, we felt alone. The few people who knew our story didn't know what to do with it, except for Jeff's best friend, Mike, who called us daily to encourage us and pray with us. A Christian co-worker also recognized that I needed a lot of prayer and emotional support. She promised to walk with me through the pain and to pray daily for Jeff and me.

During that painful season I began to fight for my marriage. I had not asked God to help me forgive Jeff, but my heart significantly began to soften.

The first step toward healing began when I tried to understand my husband's struggle with pornography. I started meeting with a Christian counselor and was shocked to learn how many Christian men, including pastors, struggle with porn. I learned that the term *sexual addiction* wasn't an excuse for lack of self-control, but a real and growing problem among both unchurched and churched men and women. Most important, I read of marriages that had rebounded after a pornography revelation. I began to wonder, *Is it possible that God could make something beautiful out of this mess?* For the first time, I felt as if there was hope.

While we were making progress in our marriage, we were getting nowhere finding new jobs or selling our home. After three months of waiting, we decided to go ahead and move to North Carolina. As frightening as it was to move to a new state with no job prospects, Jeff and I were desperate for a new start.

Our transition to North Carolina was incredibly smooth. Within a matter of weeks we both found jobs and our house in Buffalo sold. Our young sons adjusted to their new schools well and we finally felt like we had landed. We also found a church that we enjoyed, and slowly we began to open up about our story.

We sought out Christian counseling to continue the progress that had begun in New York. We were amazed to find that several Christian counselors in the area specialized in sexual addiction and intimacy issues. Jeff joined a Christ-centered sexual addiction group and I joined a women's Bible study for spouses of sex addicts. We were encouraged to meet couples that were experiencing victory in the wake of sexual sin. As Jeff and I began to grow closer, I started to see a light at the end of the tunnel.

Then the dam broke. A year into our recovery, a good friend of ours in Buffalo unexpectedly passed away. As I returned to our old community to attend her funeral, I felt a profound sense of sadness. Grieving her death opened a flood of emotions I had been holding back for a year. I was almost paralyzed by the pain. Like it or not, it was time for me to deal with the anger, disappointment, and hopelessness.

Working through that pain was harder than I could have imagined, but I was fortunate to have a great Christian counselor and Christian psychiatrist on my team. Jeff was also by my side. He had made tremendous strides in recovery and was ready to do whatever it took to save our marriage.

Together we grieved the consequences of Jeff's addiction and the loss of our ministry. While it felt like we were taking a huge step backward in recovery, our counselors assured us that the only way to find healing was to walk through this difficult stretch of road. I spent many days lying on the couch, staring at the wall pleading for the Lord to take away my pain. I searched the Bible looking for truth to counter the hopelessness I felt. As weary as I was from the battle, I knew I couldn't give up.

Slowly I began to feel Christ's presence. I no longer asked Him to take away the pain, but only to stay with me. Then I started to experience the Lord's healing power as He began to replace my sadness with joy. The joy was not based on my circumstances but was a result of depending on His presence.

Outside of my salvation experience, it was the most important spiritual moment of my life. Before I had known the Lord as my Savior, my Teacher, and my Friend. Now I knew Him as my Almighty Healer, Restorer of my Soul, and Mender of my Broken Heart. The experience caused me to want to share what I had learned with others who were suffering.

As we came through that dark period, Jeff and I marveled at all the resources we were finding on our recovery journey. Our counselors had given us incredible books and articles to read. We were also finding sexual addiction recovery ministries across the country via the Internet. We discovered there was a recovery subculture in the Christian community that we never knew existed. Why hadn't we found this sooner?

At the same time, we also noticed that each week new people were showing up at the addiction group and spouses' group we were attending. Our hearts went out to these families. We started to toss around the idea of putting together a list of resources we were finding for those whose world had just fallen apart. We knew from our own experience that they needed hope and support more than anything else.

As we began to put the list together, we realized that a website would allow us to link directly to all of the recovery ministries we had found online. A website would make our story very public, and we talked about the risks of being so open. In the end, we believed that we were being called to shed the light on this issue. Jeff and I began to work on the website together, and then we launched *www.porntopurity.com*.

From the start, the response was tremendous. Jeff started writing a daily blog and we recorded a few podcasts. As the hits increased, we were contacted by an Internet radio show and magazine that wanted to tell our story. Soon we were receiving emails from men and women all over the world.

While we never dreamed the website would become so popular so quickly, it shouldn't have surprised us. We know there are others out there like us—husbands who want to be free from pornography but are too ashamed to tell anyone, and wives who wonder if there is any hope. We are privileged to share our story of recovery, which is still a work in progress. While the last chapter has not yet been written, I'm excited to see how it all unfolds. Knowing that the Author of Life is at work, I know it will be a spectacular ending.

—MARSHA FISHER

*A*s with anything in marriage, a problem one spouse has is the other person's difficulty, too. While the lure and challenges of addictions can be staggering, nothing is too large for the Lord to handle, even though it's astronomical at the time to us. As we turn to Him, God can help us—and our marriages—survive the anger, mistrust, embarrassment, and pain.

Besides turning to God for wisdom, a key to overcoming the hurdles that addiction thrusts in our path, as Jeff and Marsha found, is to take advantage of Christ-honoring resources. Christian counselors and support groups can be lifesavers for marriages facing addiction or other challenges. Nothing is quite like being with people who understand what you're going through and commit to pray for you and walk with you on the journey. Perhaps that's why the Bible tells us there's wisdom in a multitude of counselors (Proverbs 15:22).

When your marriage faces a challenge, even if it seems insurmountable, take hope. God is just waiting to help you and bring others to your aid!

In Love With Another

I hadn't told my wife I loved another woman. How could I? Why would I?

After almost twenty-eight years of marriage, we'd long since removed the "D word" from our dictionary. Divorce was not an option. We often joked that neither of us wanted to train another partner. But something was different.

My parents divorced when I was three years old. In my teenage years I asked why. "We grew apart," my father said. "We didn't share as much in common."

I understood that now as an adult. Rosemary and I seemed at times to have more differences than commonalities. I liked politics; she loathed any discussion of current events. I enjoyed being home, she preferred going out. I drew energy from people; she wanted to be alone. I coveted order; she functioned in chaos.

She loved teaching children, leading the parent-teacher organizations at our daughter's school, and art. I loved football, basketball, and even baseball. She loved her cat; I loved my dog. She loved going nowhere for no particular reason at no specific time. I loved getting from point A to point B as fast as I could. She loved the journey. I loved the destination. But it didn't seem we loved each other anymore.

I knew I didn't love who I thought she'd become. I felt alone and lonely. Unappreciated. Unnoticed. Unwanted. And maybe that contributed to why I loved another woman.

I remembered the days of the years gone by. I recalled our honeymoon; the early years after we decided to grow up and old together; the first of our annual visits to the beach; when our daughter, Meaghan, was born. I remembered those times and the woman I loved then, the one I married. And I realized that I loved another woman—a woman who no longer existed.

With an age gap of eleven years, maybe it was inevitable that as we aged we'd mature at different rates. Our interests would change. Our habits would become more inflexible. Our likes and dislikes would contrast more than they would complement. But after almost three decades I realized that our marriage might be as good as it was going to get.

Still, I didn't want to settle for just a joint tax return and the same address and phone number. Rosemary often talked about what we'd do in ten years. "When Meaghan is in college or married, I want to travel."

That appealed to me. But I knew she had no clue about how discontented I was at times. Anniversaries, birthdays, and Christmases didn't seem special. The celebrations faded and we began to buy our own gifts. That was easier, at least for me. But it wasn't the life I wanted.

So I decided to write a new script. I knew I couldn't change Rosemary, so I decided to change myself.

As one year ended and another began, I didn't make promises I couldn't keep. I didn't announce any resolutions. Instead, I washed dishes. And clothes. I cooked a few meals. I marked time off on my new calendar for a couple of vacations.

I made notes weeks ahead of Valentine's Day, our anniversary, Mother's Day, and Rosemary's birthday. And although Christmas had just passed, I made notes about what to do the next year. When to put up the outdoor decorations. When to put up the tree. When to give her something unexpected.

I also made a list of projects to do at home. Some small: reframe some artwork, clean out the garage. Some large: cut down a dying tree and plant new trees, create a patio where we could relax.

But the best intentions and plans mean nothing unless implemented. So I began to do what I told myself I would do. And over the next year something wonderful happened. My wife fell in love with this other man.

–JEFF ADAMS

When we face dissatisfaction, it's easy to take the position of "Something's wrong; you need to change." When our interests pull us in opposite directions, we can just shrug and say, "We grew apart," and long for someone who seems closer. Or we can determine to close the distance. We might be able to draw closer together by determining to learn more about the areas and activities that intrigue our spouse. Or, as Jeff tried, we can think of other ways to kindle the fire, so the distances don't seem overwhelming, and so we become new people enjoying a fresh relationship. Waking up and finding a distance there doesn't mean we should make the distance greater—it gives us opportunity to close the gap and grow together.

No More Keeping Score

"Where's dinner?" my husband demanded as he burst through the front door.

"I'll be right down," I shouted from the upstairs bedroom.

Where did the time go? I had lost track of it while sorting through pictures for our twenty-fifth wedding anniversary album. Since the album was to be a surprise, I couldn't risk working on it when Mark was around.

I hastily shoved the pictures back into unmarked boxes and headed downstairs.

"Nice touch!" Mark said, pointing to the frozen chicken on the countertop. "How long did it take you to prepare that?"

The sarcasm in his voice triggered my not-so-nice response: "Did it ever cross your mind to help me fix dinner?"

Before I could snap another word, Mark grabbed his gym bag and headed for the front door. My heart raced, my palms got sweaty, and the lump in my throat stayed firmly lodged.

Hold back, I told myself. *Don't say it!*

But it was too late. The words whipped out in a vicious response. "Fine! Go to the gym like you always do."

I felt smug that I had won Round One of the "naughty versus nice" fight for the evening. But, of course, Mark had to have the final "word." He backed out of the driveway—running over the garbage can—screeching his wheels as he rounded the corner, so the neighbors could witness our not-so-private argument.

Our marriage had been reduced to a game of keeping score and one-word responses. Although I wanted to blame Mark for everything, I knew I was a key player in the breakdown of our communication. My cutting-edge remarks sliced through arguments and ignited simple discussions into full-blown attacks. Why couldn't I just keep quiet?

Tears trickled down my cheeks as I glanced at the frozen chicken. It was a painful reminder of how cold our marriage had become. After twenty-five years, we were nicer to strangers than we were to each other. I put the chicken in the refrigerator and surveyed the living room. Mark's polished wingtip shoes lay scattered across the carpet while his crisp white shirt and imported Italian suit lay in a heap on the sofa.

As I gathered them up, I remembered the care I had taken to pick out each one. Mark's shirts had to be 100 percent cotton, along with imported silk ties, hand-stitched Italian suits, and silk blend socks. He was a corporate executive with the power to destroy dreams and the lack of simple decency to treat me with respect. One of the managers of the world's largest transportation company, he carried a heavy burden. The stress of work showed in the lines on his face, the gray that covered his once-dark mustache, the creases on his forehead, and the tension in his jaw that pulsated when he got angry. Where was that nice guy I had married?

I returned upstairs to finish the work on our twenty-fifth anniversary album. Several pictures hadn't made it back in their boxes.

One of the photos was of our first date at Whitworth College in Spokane, Washington.

As I picked it up, I smiled, remembering the moment. Mark had shown up at my dorm room with a pink rosebud corsage that lay on a bed of fluorescent shreds. For weeks he had planned every detail of our date, including learning the color of my dress so he could present me with a matching corsage. That was the evening we fell in love and had our first kiss. I remembered Mark asking, "Is it okay if I kiss you?" He won my heart with that kind gesture.

Where did that man go? I wondered.

The day after our not-so-nice argument, I had lunch with my friend and prayer partner, Lynette. Her marriage had survived thirty-four years of emotional abuse, yet she stood by her man. She learned to love her husband as God directed. In a strange turn of events, he left her without warning. When I asked Lynette if she still loved Al, her response shocked me. "I love him now more than ever. I'll never give up on our marriage and I would do anything to have him back."

She gulped back sobs as she read from a letter that she never sent, which included 1 Corinthians 13:4–5, " 'Love is patient and kind. Love is not jealous or boastful or proud or rude. It does not demand its own way. It is not irritable, and it keeps no record of being wronged.' "

I zeroed in on the last phrase. "It keeps no record of being wronged." Hadn't I been doing that with Mark?

Lynette stopped reading, looked up from the letter, and asked, "What's the matter, Connie?"

I didn't hold back. I told her how the last five years of our marriage had been a series of one-word responses, zingers, and keeping score of who did what to whom. I didn't know if our marriage was salvageable.

Lynette grabbed my hands. "It's never too late. Ask God to forgive your past and envision your future together. Love doesn't keep a list of rights and wrongs."

Lynette prayed for a breakthrough in our marriage and said she would continue to pray for us.

When I got home that evening, Mark had already gone to the gym, his clothes were in their normal clump, and I found a note scribbled on the back of a gas receipt. "Gone to the gym!"

How nice of him to leave me a "love note." Even as I thought the words, I remembered what Lynette had advised: "Don't keep a list of rights and wrongs." Our marriage needed to become a team effort—not an individual sport. Scorekeepers didn't belong in a marriage relationship, and that's exactly what I had become—a scorekeeper!

That was it! I threw away the scorecard that evening and decided to surprise Mark with a duplicate of the first meal I had ever prepared for him: lasagna, salad, homemade potato rolls, and lemon meringue pie. I set the table with our wedding china, lit two white candles, and prayed, "God, bring back the 'us' in our marriage. I'm so tired of scorekeeping."

Mark returned three hours later, sweaty and tired.

"Hi, honey. Dinner is served!" I announced, not able to keep excitement out of my voice.

Mark sneered. "Sure it is. Where's the cold pizza?"

I stopped and thought, *Don't say it, Connie, don't you dare!*

"It's not pizza; it's your favorite meal." *Whew!*

Mark threw down his gym bag, washed up, and came to the table. I dimmed the lights and the candles flickered, creating a soft glow.

"What's this? It's not our anniversary," he remarked sarcastically.

The not-so-nice Connie wanted to lash back, but I remained silent. Next to Mark's plate, I placed the unfinished anniversary album with the picture of our first date pasted on the front cover. Mark held up the album with his mouth partially open as if he was about to say something, then paused. When he glanced up, tears formed in his eyes.

"Do you remember when that picture was taken?" I asked hesitantly.

"Yes, of course I do—it was our first date! I sure had a lot more hair back then, didn't I?"

I chuckled and said, "I guess you did. I think we've both changed, but we're still the same inside—right?"

Mark reached out to hug me. With tears streaking down his cheeks, he said, "Let's eat. I'm hungry!"

We both broke into laughter and held each other in a tight embrace. Mark fixed his gaze on my smile and said, "You don't mind if I kiss you, do you?"

My vision blurred with tears as I blurted out, "If you don't, I will!"

The barrier of silence had been broken and the scorecard was destroyed that evening. It's been almost ten years since our not-so-nice marriage turned into a kind, caring one. It took time and a lot of effort—especially on my part—because I had a much better memory. But slowly the scorekeeping faded as love was rekindled by date nights once a week, staying connected through the day by frequent phone calls, and problem-solving together by learning to listen and not react.

There are no winners or losers in our marriage—just a couple in love who has learned to not keep score!

–CONNIE K. POMBO

When asked the secret to a happy marriage, one man responded, "Just be nice to each other." It's so easy to use our mouths as weapons. And sometimes we can feel so satisfied to shoot a witty zinger . . . to use clever words to inflict pain when we're feeling an emotional sting ourselves. As Connie found out, it's relatively easy to get in the habit of being mean—to be nicer to everyone else than to the person who should be our best friend. We forget that when we hurt our mate, we're not just making a basket on a verbal court with words that will bounce away. It's more like shooting an arrow at the thoughts and feelings of the one we love—an arrow that will stick and hurt.

When we wound our partner, we handicap our marriage, and we inflict injury on ourselves in the process. When we're nice to our mate, we're ultimately nicer to everyone we encounter—including ourselves.

My Cheating Heart

You're not going to get all religious on me now, are you?"

His words ambushed my defenses. My head and heart had been wandering headlong into an affair. These words forced me to stop and survey my situation.

We had been co-workers for a few years. And until we were placed on the same team, I hadn't even really noticed him.

Then a special project came up. I was passionate about it and requested to be a part of the initiative. The other members on the team were assigned to it by default. This was not a career-advancing move for any of us. It wasn't even that high on the upper management's list of priorities. However, if we succeeded, we would change the status quo for our colleagues. I was willing to do whatever it took to ensure triumph.

While I was venturing into new territory in my profession, my husband's career was advancing and his trip to the top was impressive. He worked long hours during the week and took a couple of night classes, so I was home alone with the children during the evenings. He spent quality time with the kids on the weekends, while I poured that time and energy into my project.

I had no problem putting in extra hours on the weekends—even on Sundays. My family had stopped going to church when I was in high school, and my husband had only attended sporadically as a child, so neither of us pushed for an early Sunday morning wake-up call. It was our day of rest—or at least a day for catching a few extra hours of sleep to fuel our professional frenzy.

When my work project first started, management carved out daily time for us to plan, prepare, and implement our strategies. But after a year, budget cuts loomed and they decided to abandon the project. Our team agreed to continue the project on our own time.

Time. The fuel for relationships.

My time was siphoned away from family and into a business partnership. Our team attended conferences regarding our project—day conferences, weekend conferences, and then a weeklong conference out of town.

We had time for chatter on trips to and from conferences. Our professional team began to share personal details of our lives. We shared meals and recreational time. I began to spend more time with team members than with my family.

Next came little expressions of caring—a hug to comfort, a touch of the hand to encourage, a caress, a kiss. A look exchanged, dreams shared, frustrations aired. My personal friendship with one team member began to evolve into an emotional and physical relationship.

One weekend my family and I went to church to see my daughter sing a duet with her best friend, who attended the church. When I returned to work the next day, I mentioned my church visit—thus the words, "You're not going to get all religious on me now, are you?"

Even though I didn't go to church every Sunday, I actually did think of myself as religious. Others also considered me religious. Yet this man who was stealing my heart didn't.

This one trip to church and these words brought my long-held values back into focus. They sharply contrasted how I was living. I had strayed from my commitment to Christ, but He knew where to find me.

Jesus, the one I had accepted as Savior in my youth, is the Good Shepherd, leaving the ninety-nine to go after the one. But I came to know Him during this time as the "hound of heaven." I could not break free of His dogged pursuit.

And His messages came from the most unlikely sources.

For instance, an associate approached me one day. She worked in my department, yet our paths rarely crossed. She walked into my office and said, "The decisions you are making could destroy your family. I say this because I care about you."

Then she turned and walked out. Who did she think she was, and what did she think she knew? I wondered.

I realized that yes, my behavior had the potential to destroy my family. Heaven's hound had pursued me into a corner and was forcing me to make a choice.

Our team was selected to travel abroad for three weeks. I knew that this would be a pivotal point in my clandestine relationship.

Three weeks. Twenty-one days. Foreign countries. Uncharted territory in an illicit affair. Would I step over the line or draw a line?

I could see two ways out of my corner. I could confess to my husband and ask for forgiveness—letting him decide what he wanted to do with my cheating heart. Or I could begin planning a new life with a man who appeared to adore me. Either way, the truth seemed determined to come out. I couldn't hide any longer.

My back was up against a wall. Telling the truth would most likely lead to a divorce, while choosing a new life with another man would require a divorce. I couldn't blame my husband if he left and took the children. My actions had given away my rights to be a part of the family we had created together.

I wished I could go back a couple of years and make better choices. I wanted to go back to being the family we had been before. However, actions have consequences. I was going to have to face the ones I had invited.

I called my husband and asked him to come home from work so we could talk. I arranged for the children to go to my parents' house.

I told my husband the extent of my relationship with the other man, and I asked for his forgiveness. Now he had a decision to make.

We both shed a lot of tears that day.

To my astonishment, I received undeserved forgiveness. He chose to forgive me that day, but the consequences of my actions did not disappear.

Our relationship was severely damaged. The total trust he had always extended was shattered. He had questions and I owed him honest answers—answers that exposed things about me that I surely did not want to reveal, like pride, insecurity, and shameful actions.

Pride had convinced me that I would never need to worry about infidelity.

Insecurities had haunted me. For years I questioned whether I was enough—pretty enough, smart enough, sexy enough—to keep my husband's attention. And I'd felt left behind as his career advanced.

Most of all, my actions shamed me. My once unblemished reputation was now tarnished beyond recognition.

My husband accepted me, and Jesus continued to pursue me by placing me in the chair of a hairdresser who became my spiritual mentor. Our family started searching for a church home.

Luke 7:47 says, "I tell you, her sins—and they are many—have been forgiven, so she has shown me much love. But a person who is forgiven little shows only little love."

I had been forgiven much. Therefore, I began to love much. My husband's love was an example of Christ's love and forgiveness. Instead of running from the hound of heaven, I turned and embraced Him. For the first time in my life, I no longer thought of myself as religious, but redeemed!

Marriage had always been high on my priority list. How had I strayed so far away from the beliefs I held so dear? I had never intended to get involved with another man.

Obviously, my intentions and my actions did not match up. I had been careless. And Satan can do a lot of damage with carelessness as he seeks to kill, steal, and destroy. I acknowledged for the first time the existence of my enemy and his agenda.

I began to seek ways to intentionally protect my marriage. On a Christian radio station I heard a speaker talk about his marital safety boundaries. His boundaries addressed the very areas I had neglected. I vowed to adopt them as my own.

From that day on, I would not ride in a car, travel, meet behind closed doors, or share meals alone with someone of the opposite gender. Any warning signals in my head were to be heeded, not ignored.

I realized that over time I had become desensitized by what I was seeing and hearing. As an avid reader and a hopeless romantic, I realized my need to censor what was going into my mind. I stopped reading novels, watching movies or television shows, or listening to music that set unrealistic expectations for romantic love or glorified unhealthy relationships. I began to build a hedge of protection around my marriage.

Some people have called my hedge unnecessary and downright silly. Nevertheless, my intentions are now being sustained by my actions, and I am honoring my marriage and my husband.

—TONYA BROWN

*T*he Bible tells us that a person who thinks he or she is standing should be careful not to fall (1 Corinthians 10:12). None of us means to be smug. We just think we'll never fall into any traps—like adultery.

That's why we all need to make sure we're taking steps to protect our marriage, as Tonya learned to do. This is a great exercise for a couple to do together—to make a list of ways we can make sure we don't fall into insidious emotional, relational, or physical traps. To develop safeguards together. And to make sure we keep our lines of communication clear— like mentioning when the old college flame has emailed us or when a co-worker seems to be trying to get us alone. With such open communication, a couple can discuss things that may send up red flags, and they can find solutions together.

Marriages face onslaughts from every direction. As we stand together, we can keep our union protected from subtle or obvious dangers.

A Gift With Priceless Wrapping

Much joy and happiness has come to our marriage, but not in the way I expected: packaged neatly in beautiful paper and tied with a perfect bow.

I left college determined to set the world on fire as a career woman. I grew up in a solid home led by a domineering father. I learned to be a high achiever and a perfectionist.

Then I met him—tall, dark-haired, self-assured, and an all-state athlete in two sports. He had an easygoing personality and was never at a loss for friends. I admired him so much.

I was short, redheaded, and competitive—a type-A personality who was too busy achieving to have many friends. The human wrappings each of us was gifted with worked both for and against our marriage. He spent his time loving me just the way I was, but eventually saying in no uncertain terms that he wanted my time minus all my multi-tasking. I spent my time in those first years loving him ferociously, but also entertaining thoughts of "if only . . ."

If only he made more money . . . if only he acted like . . . if only, if only, if only . . . I was always committed to Donald Davidson and never once thought of divorce, but I certainly made myself restless in our marriage.

One time joy came to our marriage wrapped in a cloth-covered table laden with twenty kinds of tasty morsels and an outstanding centerpiece. When the last of our many guests had gone, I basked in the glow of those who'd oohed and ahhed and given me a hundred compliments—not only about the food, but also about my house and my hostess skills.

Don and I had tidied up and stored the leftovers when he requested, "Sit a few minutes with me."

For once I didn't do all the talking.

"It was a wonderful party and you did an outstanding job," he said, "but I like it best when there's just two or three couples so I can really have a conversation with them."

That didn't stop all large gatherings; however, I learned we were both happier if I consulted with him first.

Then came the time in our lives when I became a stay-at-home mom to our two children. My professional attire changed to mom jeans and an oversized T-shirt. I barely had time to brush my teeth, let alone put on makeup. One day our children and I delivered a surprise birthday cake to Don's office. The women working there were definitely packaged attractively.

After that I never lazed around in a robe, throwing on clothes just before my husband came from work. The effort paid off! One day Don exclaimed, "Zeta, you always look great; I feel like you look good just for me."

From the hour of our wedding, I learned quickly that the package Don liked best was me, without wrapping. One day I stepped out of the shower while he was lying on our bed. It probably had happened many times before, but this time he put it into words. "You have no idea how you turn me on."

I thought, *This man can never get enough sex!*

When I told him that, a huge smile spread across his face as he answered, "You're right about that!"

A line I'd read immediately filled my mind: "Women give sex to get affection; men give affection to get sex." I'm not sure this is entirely true, but I do know if sex permeates my husband's mind, being held, hugged, and kissed definitely helps me be more passionate.

Another package I discovered the hard way was the one wrapped with printed words all over the paper. I just expected Don to know what a great husband I thought he was; what a great dad I thought he was; what a great employee he was; and what a great lover he was.

You might say I stumbled onto this wrapping paper. I will never forget the appreciation I saw in his eyes when I expressed just one admiring thought. I decided that day that the power of affirming words spoken honestly can wrap a marriage as much as arms wrapped in a wonderful hug.

Then there was the "be kind" wrapping paper. The Lord himself spoke so quietly in my thoughts. "Why are you so agreeable and polite in public to your friends and mere acquaintances, but you frump around at home, yelling and not caring how your words sound?"

Without hesitation, I resolved to follow the Scripture, "I need your help, especially in my own home, where I long to act as I should" (Psalm 101:2 TLB).

Oh, and then there's been my life, wrapped in busyness with no time for my marriage to be tied with a bow. Even my daughter noticed it; she started saying, "I'm going to 'play Dad' now and tell you to stop going to meetings, meetings, meetings."

I've always loved the challenge of being overbooked. After the kids got in school and I went back to teaching, I taught classes all day, followed by Monday night Delta Kappa Gamma meeting,

Tuesday night PTA, Wednesday night women's Bible study at church, Thursday night writers' group meeting . . . you get the idea.

And all the time without realizing it, my husband spelled love T-I-M-E. He never asked, "Will you please make me as important as a meeting?" but eventually I caught the idea; the best way for me to have a totally untalkative, disgruntled husband stomping around was to overbook myself.

One year our marriage was wrapped in the want ads and the local supermarket ads. For the first time after eighteen years of marriage, my husband was jobless—when his company was sold. We had no company car, no life insurance, and no health insurance.

I wondered, *What am I doing to boost his self-esteem during this toughest of times?*

So during my devotional time, I asked God to reveal more ways I could show love. As a result, I learned to share Don's excitement even when I didn't feel it; I thanked Don for making me the most important thing in his life; I assured him and assured him we would make it through and that he was no less a person because his career had been chopped; I shopped the ads and found menus to prepare from the most frugal foods. We learned to celebrate small successes such as excellent interviews. And we learned that uncertain times are better with laughter and passion.

We learned to tithe whatever money God sent our way, to value each other's opinions and thoughts, and to pray together and for each other.

Sometimes I think of our marriage as gift wrapped in a bag with layers of tissue paper that represent four decades of life committed to marriage and to each other. One thickness of tissue is taking time to look into each other's eyes when we talk. Another is saying thank-you for making life pleasurable.

Another tissue paper, probably colored red, might represent caution so only one of us speaks at a time, and for me to remember not to interrupt! An orange tissue could portray avoiding words like "you never" and "you always," which helps us be truthful in our disagreements.

My marriage worked until its final gift box. Cancer claimed Don's life when he was sixty-two. I didn't have the opportunity for us to be a white-haired couple holding hands together. I also was not caught in the scenario of hurriedly wrapping up our lives together—we had time to say and do many, many things before his death.

My marriage was not always wrapped in beautiful paper and tied with a perfect bow, but the gift of its blessings makes me urge all married couples to seek hope, and to continually "try again" to achieve a fascinating, fulfilling life together.

—ZETA DAVIDSON

Though our marriages may come wrapped differently, marriage is a gift. It's a present bestowed by a gracious God on people He loves. We know the story of the original marriage—how Adam had his Creator to talk with each day. But he longed to have a bit of that love and companionship in skin—an equal walking along the earth's pass with him.

Adam maybe didn't know what was causing the unrest in his spirit. But God saw it wasn't good for him to be alone with nothing to relate to but the animals (Genesis 2). And when God presented Eve to him, he certainly understood that he was receiving an incomparable gift!

How often do we think of marriage as a blessing from the Lord? If we regularly pause to think of it as His special gift to us, well, it might just help us appreciate what we have!

The Krikit Caper

Honey! Would you come in here please?" my husband called from another room. "Krikit, too. Here girl! Come here!"

Hearing these words, I left my work in the kitchen and walked to the bedroom where my husband was waiting. Our little dog, a four-pound black toy poodle named Krikit, hopped off of the couch where she had been sleeping and followed me.

My husband met us at the door and asked us to sit. I sat down on the edge of the bed. Krikit hopped up on the bed and sat down beside me. We both looked at him, giving him our complete attention.

Just three months earlier, my husband and I had married. We had met the previous year, fallen in love, and pledged before our family, friends, and the Lord to love and cherish each other for the rest of our lives.

But learning to live with another person can be challenging. We lived in a very small house with a very small bedroom. Consequently, in order to have any space between our bed and our dresser, the bed was pushed against a wall. The room was also adjacent to a small bathroom. Unfortunately, I had formed the habit of walking out of the bathroom after a shower with a towel wrapped around my wet hair.

Then, standing in front of the dresser and mirror, I would unwrap the towel from around my hair and drop it on the bed as I began to brush my hair and blow it dry. The side of the bed where my wet towel always landed happened to be my husband's side. So many nights he ended up crawling into a bed that was damp and cold.

My husband had asked me many times if I would please alter my routine such that my wet towel was *not* dropped on his side of the bed. But somehow, I never seemed to be able to remember his request. My actions were by no means intentional, but his bed ended up damp and cold just the same. Every time he said something to me about it, I responded with good intentions—but I had formed a routine, and a habit is hard to break.

So there we were, Krikit and I, sitting in rapt attention, all four eyes on my husband. He moved from the door closer to us. Standing in front of us, he began to speak.

"I am afraid I need to talk to the two of you about a serious matter," he said solemnly. "It has come to my attention that one of you has been leaving a wet towel on the bed. Now, I don't know which one of you has been doing this . . . and I don't need to know." He continued earnestly, gesturing as he spoke. "I would just like the behavior to stop."

I chuckled as I began to apologize, but he waved me away saying, "Uh-uh! I don't need to hear any confessions from either one of you. In fact, it would probably be better if I don't ever know which one is the guilty party. I would just like the behavior stopped, please."

I burst out laughing and kissed him. It was such an amusing way for him to get his point across. And it worked. Never again did I drop a wet towel on his side of the bed. From then on, every time I unwrapped my hair and started to drop my towel on the bed, I remembered my funny husband and chuckled as I walked to the bathroom to hang it on the towel rack.

That was thirty years ago. My husband and I are still happily married. Like any couple we have had our ups and downs, but we are still glad to have each other. We still tease about that funny episode. Many times through the years, we have told each other of some new negative behavior that we suspected Krikit may have been guilty of (or whatever other pet we had at the time). She has been suspected of many infractions, such as leaving the cap off of the toothpaste, not cleaning the sink after she shaved, and forgetting to leave phone messages. Why, once she was even suspected of parking the car crooked in the garage, making it difficult for one of us to get our other car in the garage!

I still remember with fondness my new husband's amusing method for changing my behavior. Climbing into a cold, damp bed at night after a hard day's work was surely more than frustrating, especially after repeated requests for me to stop. He could so easily have handled it with anger instead of humor. But he chose a better way, and it worked.

—HARRIET MICHAEL

As Harriet found, the big problem for newlyweds—and even longer-weds—is learning to live together. It's not the big sacrifices but the little annoyances that are more likely to rip apart the cloak of companionship.

The Bible indicates that laughter is a medicine, and that's certainly true in marriage. No matter what ills a marriage faces—from the small, daily irritations to the big challenges—everything goes better with a little humor. Laughter diffuses things that could otherwise be explosive.

Seeing humor in situations isn't a natural gift for most of us. We have to learn to open our eyes to the zany, crazy, and ludicrous elements in our circumstances. We have to purposely find something to laugh about.

But as we learn to laugh together, it not only creates a sense of playfulness and a new perspective, but also buoys our marriage, helping us keep afloat no matter where the waves of life may toss us.

Dollar-Store Romance

I almost killed my wife last week. There weren't any weapons in the area, and I would certainly never lay a hand on her, but I thought for sure a call to 9-1-1 was only moments away.

What caused this near-fatality? A balloon. Actually, a bunch of balloons, but I'm pretty sure just one of them would have done the trick.

It all started rather innocently. At work the day before, I was walking past the receptionist's desk when I saw her struggling with a balloon on the end of a stick.

"I know I probably shouldn't ask," I said, "but what's the balloon for?"

"Today is Suzie's birthday," she replied, "and I'm in charge of decorating."

"But why is the balloon on a stick?"

"Because I thought it was cool and just something different."

She was right. The balloon on the stick looked vaguely like a mutated rose on a stem. Now, I've never been accused of being very artistic or spontaneous, but at that moment one of those cartoon light bulbs must have appeared over my head. Inspiration had struck! If she thought it was fun and exciting, surely my wife would think so, too.

Normally being a mild-mannered, low-key type of guy, I was about to venture into the world of "creative romance," which was a scary, foreign concept to me. But I was now committed to the challenge.

I learned I could get the balloons at the dollar store just across the street. I quickly calculated that would probably be in the range of my cash on-hand, so my quest had begun. Surely my lovely wife of over twenty-five years was worth a shopping spree in the dollar store.

I headed for the kids' party section. Batman napkins, no. Barbie plates, no. Pirate hat, no. There they were. Eight balloon-on-a-stick party favors per package for just one dollar. I had hit the jackpot. But if eight was good, I reasoned, then sixty-four would be that much better. You can never have too many balloons, can you?

I grabbed several packs and headed for the checkout with unbridled glee. I had planned to take the next day off from work, so Operation Surprise My Wife was underway.

The next morning I kissed my wife at the door as she headed off to work. When I saw the car drive away, I ripped open the balloon packages and started blowing up the "flowers" that would make up my beautiful bouquet. Who needs a florist?

The tricky part was tying the balloons to the little disks that would be shoved into the sticks, but I was not to be denied. Out of breath from excessive blowing and with my fingertips aching from fighting with the balloons, I now needed to find a vase, and the logical place to look was under the kitchen sink. Voilà! That one back in the corner would work just fine.

Now the first glitch in my plan reared its ugly head. When I looked at one balloon at a time, it didn't look all that big. But when

I tried to get sixteen of them on two-foot-long sticks arranged in a single vase, it suddenly seemed like I was struggling with a fleet of blimps. And what would I do with all these extra balloons?

For the first time, I wondered if this was such a great idea. Maybe I should have gone to the florist after all. My wife would probably prefer real flowers, and balloons don't even smell nice. Maybe this spontaneous, creative romance stuff was just for newlyweds.

I decided if this was going to be a catastrophe, it might as well be a gigantic one. I went to the party store and found those pin-together letters so I could make a personalized "I Love You" sign to hang over the living room. A roll of pink ribbon to wrap around the vase completed my shopping, and I rushed home to finish my decorating.

Finally I was done. My bouquet looked fabulous, and big. The "I Love You" banner was perfect, although it did sag a little more than I expected. And all the extra balloons had been randomly scattered around the living room, including one on each of the ceiling fan blades.

On second thought, maybe it was simply tacky. Maybe this whole idea would crash down around me when my wife saw dozens of multi-colored spheres bobbing on sticks from every conceivable nook of the living room. But the sound of a car pulling up out front signaled the moment of truth.

The door opened, my wife walked in, and that's when I almost killed her. Her eyes got big, her mouth dropped open, and I thought she was about to drop dead from the shock. But when her breath came back, she erupted into the loudest laughter I'd heard in quite a while.

"I love it!" she screamed as she surveyed the room. "I love it! This is great! Where's the camera? Nobody will believe this! And it's not even a special occasion. Wow! This is the best surprise I've ever had!"

Suddenly, my bouquet didn't seem so tacky. It's a memory neither of us will forget. She couldn't believe I had done it all by myself, and all just for her.

And I'll remember the complete joy in her face. I was reminded it doesn't take expensive jewelry, exotic vacations, or fancy clothes to create special moments and express love. You don't even need to have a special reason—just a little imagination and a lot of desire to celebrate love.

I don't profess to be an expert in relationship building or how to be a perfect spouse. But I have learned that even the simplest act, even as easy as blowing up a bunch of balloons, can express the depths of love for your mate and put a sparkle in her eye. I was able to do it with a little dollar-store romance.

—JEFF FRIEND

The little things in life count—especially in the area of marriage. Romance doesn't consist only of big splashes of elaborately expensive surprises. As Jeff learned, it can be as thrifty as a dollar-store surprise, or whatever your budget can afford!

The best gifts can be small, fun feats just to show that we were thinking of the one we love. The gift of romance can come wrapped in tidbits of thoughtfulness and creativity. What impresses the one we love is that we took time out of a busy schedule to think of him or her and to focus on doing something fun and special.

Making Room for Daddy

I want my mommy!" screamed our five-year-old, breaking free of his daddy and bolting out of the haunted house into my awaiting arms.

I comforted our trembling child, searching for my husband, but when our eyes met, the pain in his expression broke my heart. What we had planned as a long-needed family night out had ended with his feeling even more alienated from his children.

All the next day, that recollection bothered me. Our son ran to me because he didn't understand Daddy could protect him, Daddy could hold him. My husband had become an outsider, a weekend visitor who simply brought home the paycheck. Because Dad wasn't available, our children had compensated by becoming more dependent on me. Experiences like we'd had at the carnival were painful reminders that this family wasn't whole.

As the owner-operator of a business, my husband spent many nights on the road, or came and went before the children woke up in the morning. We'd become so accustomed to his long absences that we seldom included him in excursions or asked his help for anything more than changing the oil in the car or mowing the grass. Though I rationalized that this gave him more free time to rest, in reality, we had divorced him emotionally.

The next time our daughter brought a broken toy for me to fix, I decided to do things differently. I suggested she take it to Daddy, even though I could reassemble the favorite plaything with my eyes closed, since it came apart so regularly. Her incredulous expression further confirmed my realization that we had been unconsciously shutting him out of our daily lives. Watching him labor over the project, I realized it would not be easy to bring him back in.

I prayed for perseverance in becoming a more supportive partner. Since so much of what I did was routine, it was hard to delegate those responsibilities. I had to consciously evaluate whether it was important who did the task. As I surrendered more and more to my husband, I recognized that I'd played a big part in the problem by making myself a martyr.

We began working as a team, and our parenting became more balanced. His objectivity balanced my emotional intuition, and our children benefited the most from this change in family government. And as I included my husband in more routine decisions, he took more of an interest in me, becoming my best advocate. Both our marriage and my self-image improved.

As I started reinforcing that Daddy's love was spoken in different ways, and pointing out to the kids that when we did something special it was because of his sacrifice, our children began to respect him as more than just a breadwinner. They learned that love included commitment and working when you'd rather play.

The kids started saving special papers and school experiences to share. When something funny happened we helped each other "remember to tell Dad." By the time he got home, they were bursting with stories. And as their father felt more important in their lives, he worked to make his schedule accommodate more of their activities.

At first, giving up this power was hard for me. My whole identity revolved around my role as Super Mom.

Our roles reversed when I went away to a weeklong conference, leaving my children in Dad's capable hands. As our daughter rehashed a disappointing test experience, and our son shared his news to sustain his homesick mom, I felt that pain of being an outsider. But then I received flowers and a card proclaiming how proud they were of me, signed by all of them. I realized my choices had not been sacrifices but rather good investments.

Those difficult years now seem far removed. I no longer have to orchestrate situations to make my husband feel needed, for our children have come to depend on his good judgment and common sense. They are becoming people of integrity because of his example. He bolsters my patience when I'm frazzled and becomes my knight in shining armor when I'm scared or discouraged.

"Make room for Dad!" demands our youngest, as he joins the family at our beach house table to play cards. And when my husband's eye catches mine, his sparkle warms me. I'm thankful for all those investments, and for the memories yet to be made with our grandchildren.

                                        —ROBERTA UPDEGRAFF

~

A wise woman builds her home," Proverbs 14:1 tells us. But this is also true for men. A wise spouse keeps an eye on the overall scope of the family. And a wise spouse realizes that he or she has a lot to do with the attitudes the children have toward his or her mate. Because of time or personality, one parent is often more naturally able to connect with the kids than the other. But to have a well-balanced family, the par-

ent with this knack can act as a liaison to help the other parent and kids connect.

This doesn't just benefit the kids. When a family is strong, a marriage is strong!

The Shoes No One Can Fill

As I walked through the dimly lit house one evening, I stumbled across my husband's size-13 black tennis shoes. I crashed to the floor, taking with me several picture frames from the coffee table.

"Why can't he put his shoes in the closet?" I mumbled. "He knows I hate tripping over them."

Just then my husband yelled from the back of the house, "What's all the racket about? Are you okay?"

That did it.

"No, I'm *not* okay!" I hollered. "Not okay at all!"

Stan came to the door of the room and stared at me. I could tell he wanted to laugh, but he didn't. "What happened?" he asked innocently.

"Why can't you just put your stupid shoes in the closet, like normal people?" I grumbled, sitting up to inspect my wounds.

"Well, it might help if you'd turn a light on instead of wandering through the house in the dark," he said, smugly.

"That's beside the point, Stan. You know I've asked you dozens of times to stop leaving your shoes all over the house; they're like two sailboats. I'm serious; they're dangerous."

We stared silently at each other across the floor.

"I don't leave my shoes scattered everywhere, and I don't ask you to put them in the closet, either," I said, unwilling to get on with my life. "So why should I have to put yours away?"

He reached for the shoes and disappeared down the hall. I knew they'd be back. It was only a matter of time.

Later in the week, I arrived home and discovered five pairs of Stan's shoes in the living room.

His house shoes camped under the edge of the couch.

His work shoes decorated the hearth.

His ugly brown dress shoes jutted out from under the coffee table.

His high-tops lay in front of the rocker.

And those abominable black tennis shoes glared at me from in front of the grandfather clock.

Scowling at the slew of shoes, I had a malicious idea. Starting at one end of the living room, I placed all ten shoes in a straight line until they reached the hallway. I stood back and admired my work. He wouldn't be able to get through the room without having to walk over them—or move them.

That'll serve him right, I said to myself. *Let him see what it's like to maneuver around these boats. Better yet, let him see what it's like to have to put them all in the shoe rack.*

I waited for his arrival home with much anticipation, but the parade of shoes didn't seem to faze him.

"What's this?" was all he said. The next time I looked, the shoes were gone. Still, I knew they'd be back. They always came back.

One day after driving my daughter to school, I returned home, made myself a cup of coffee, and settled on the couch for a time of devotion. I would try to ignore the familiar size-13 shoes scattered all over the room, but it was difficult. As I read from Thessalonians,

I laughed out loud when my eyes came to rest on this verse: "Rejoice evermore" (1 Thessalonians 5:16 KJV).

"God," I said wearily, "if you can give me one good reason to rejoice over these shoes, I'll be happy to do so. Just one, Lord!"

Early the next morning, I drove Stan to the airport. He was flying from Houston to Baltimore for the weekend to participate in the firefighters' annual muscular dystrophy softball tournament.

"Have a good time," I said, giving him a kiss at the gate. "See you Monday." He waved me off.

I returned home late in the afternoon, switched on the radio, and started preparing dinner. Suddenly I heard a voice saying, "Once again, there are no survivors in that plane crash."

For a moment, my heart stopped. I sat down at the kitchen table, my hands shaking. *Plane crash? What plane crash? Oh, God, no!*

But the news was over. Fumbling frantically with the dial, I found another station and heard the tragic details: USAir Flight 427 from Chicago to Pittsburgh had gone down, killing all passengers on board.

Shocked by the news, I laid my head on the cold table and sobbed, both from relief and sadness. Even though my husband was not on that plane, I was jolted to realize how uncertain life is, and how numbing the shock must be for those families who had loved ones aboard.

That evening, after putting my daughter to bed, I stooped to remove Stan's black tennis shoes from where he'd left them in front of the full-length mirror. But instead of putting them away, I put them on. They felt awkward and massive on my small feet.

For several minutes I studied my ridiculous reflection in the mirror. Then I looked down at the shoes. They were molded in the exact shape of my husband's feet. I knew every hump and bump so well.

No one else could wear these shoes but Stan. How would I feel if I knew my husband would never again fill these shoes? The thought was unthinkable. Somewhere tonight a woman, without warning, was a widow. Her husband would never again wear his shoes. A chill sliced through my heart. I mourned for her.

The day Stan came home, our daughter, Anna Marie, and I gathered in the living room to hear all the details of his trip—of how his team had been undefeated in their division.

While my daughter admired the shiny, first-place trophy Stan pulled proudly from his bag, I couldn't keep my eyes off the size-13 shoes he'd dropped beneath the coffee table. Funny, I didn't wish them to be anywhere else. And I vowed to never complain about them again. They would always be a comforting sign to me. My husband was home.

—DAYLE ALLEN SHOCKLEY

We're not in a marriage very long before we find our own "big shoes" that are likely to trip us—after all, minor irritations come in all sizes! And the closer we are to someone and the more time we spend with him or her, the more likely we are to see and focus on their imperfections. It's enough to trip up the best of marriages!

Sometimes we have to learn, as Dayle did, to look at the small annoyances in light of the big picture. What does it really matter in the light of love, life, and eternity? As we train ourselves to remember how fleeting our years together may be, those niggling aggravations fall into their proper perspective.

Our Honeymoon and the Dangers of the Demon Brew

Linda and I had been engaged for two years when we decided to get married. I was the ripe old age of twenty-one and Linda was nineteen—mere pups. I was so nervous at our wedding that I forgot the name of one of my groomsmen.

After the ceremony we jumped in my poppy red '64 ½ Mustang. With a legion of cars following us, and a bumper of cans announcing our glad marriage tidings, we raced through the streets of Kansas City. Later we changed clothes and headed for our honeymoon destination—the glorious metropolis of Columbia, Missouri, population 20,000.

A two-hour drive brought us to the parking lot of the luxurious Holiday Inn. We smiled at each other as we got out of the car.

Summing up my courage before the desk clerk, I barely got the words out. "We need a room for tonight."

I was hoping he would ask me if we were married so I could proudly boast that we were. He didn't.

Instead, he said, "I'm sorry, sir. We have no rooms."

"None? Is there another hotel or motel nearby?"

The clerk made several phone calls. "The problem is that all the rooms in Columbia are filled," he explained. "There's a big gun convention going on this weekend. You should have made reservations."

His chide devastated my manhood as the new husband and protector of my wife. My lack of organization ruined our honeymoon. I leaned over to the desk clerk, talking low so Linda could not hear me.

"Well, you see, we just got married and we need a place to stay."

"I'm sorry, but I don't think . . ." He paused in mid-sentence, then said, "I've got an idea."

The clerk dialed the phone one more time. "Oh good. You do have a room left. I'm sending a young, newly married couple over to you."

The sympathetic clerk leaned over the counter and in low tones said, "Well, it's not the best place, but at least you have somewhere to stay for the night. It's called the Tiger Inn Hotel in Old Town."

Talk about one relieved husband—I know how Joseph must have felt about two thousand years earlier. Pulling into the Tiger Inn Hotel lot, we saw a dirty brick multi-story building that had to have been built before the turn of the twentieth century—maybe even the Civil War.

The lobby looked like a scene from *Sunset Boulevard*. The windows were covered with faded drapes that had large flowers on them. I figured bootleggers in the 1920s probably saw those same flowers.

Our room was on the seventh floor. Fortunately, they had an

elevator. We opened the door to a small and extraordinarily dingy room, which was more like a large cubicle. As terrible as it was, it was better than squishing into our poppy red Mustang on our honeymoon night.

I took Linda in my arms and kissed her tenderly. At that moment, nothing mattered—not the room, not our hotel. Nothing but the joy of the two of us being together. At that moment reality hit me. We were married. We were committed to each other for the rest of our lives. That's what mattered.

While Linda got ready for bed, I went to buy a small bottle of champagne, about the size of a Coke bottle. (These were my days before accepting Christ, so I didn't see any problem with this; later I would find it was my downfall.)

When she came out of the bathroom, I poured a glass of champagne for each of us. We toasted each other and kissed again. Then I got ready for bed.

I walked out of the bathroom a new man, expecting a warm and friendly greeting. Instead, I heard gentle snoring coming from the bed. Linda was asleep. I tried to wake her. As she rolled back to sleep she could only mumble, "Oh, I'm so tired. I think the champagne did me in."

No! This can't be happening—not on top of everything else. This is not the way a wedding night is supposed to be! I thought as I vigorously shook her again. No luck. One small glass of champagne mixed with an exhausting week of wedding preparation and Linda was out like a drunken sailor.

Wow, had I made a mistake! I sat there for the longest time, vowing never to touch the demon brew again. Finally I turned on the black-and-white 14-inch TV and watched some movie. This was not the honeymoon I wanted.

The next morning Linda and I went to breakfast at a Big Boy restaurant. I was exhilarated to look at my young, beautiful wife across the table from me. I felt I had stepped into a new plateau in life. The marvelous thing was that I'd stepped into this new phase of life with the woman I loved.

We left Columbia and headed for Linda's parents' cabin at the Lake of the Ozarks, about 120 miles away. We got there in the late afternoon after getting lost only twice in the winding hills of the Ozarks' unmarked country roads.

We walked down the hill from the cabin to the lake. It was on one of the main waterways so we watched a lot of boats and skiers. For supper, we walked up a steep hill to the only gathering spot in this small Ozark town. They had a jukebox and served a little bit of food. Later in the evening, numerous couples came up to dance to western music.

We turned in early but couldn't go to sleep—but not because of romantic reasons! Rustic cabins in the woods, like bootlegger hotel rooms, aren't known for being overly comfortable. About two in the morning, we lay under the open window on that warm spring night. I heard a heavy thud outside in the bushes. It sounded like something really big was moving around the cabin.

"Did you hear that?" I asked Linda. After all, it was *her* parents' cabin.

"Yeah."

"Have you heard anything like that down here before?"

Linda shook her head no. We both raised our heads to the windowsill and carefully scanned the horizon. There was no moon so it was very dark. We saw a lot of dark shadows in the woods.

Resting our heads back on the pillows, we tried again to go to sleep. *Thud.* There was that loud noise again! And again! And another time!

I flew out of the bed and ran to the door. I tentatively stepped out but could see nothing.

"Mike, come on back," Linda said. "It's probably okay."

Linda's calm dismissal of the noise reassured me. After all, she'd stayed at this cabin plenty of times. I stretched out and was almost asleep when a shrill scream came from the woods.

Both of us popped out of the bed like someone had tied rockets to our backs.

I reacted first. I tried to sound unworried but I think the shaking in my voice gave me away. "So what do you think about going back to Kansas City?"

"I think it would be great. Let's leave right now."

We threw our clothes in our suitcase, turned out the lights, and in five minutes were out the door. We were glad to leave that spooky place. On the trip back, we remarked how refreshing a hot shower would feel when we got to our new apartment.

At 5 a.m. I opened the door to the beckoning warmth of our small apartment. "I'll take a shower first and then you can follow," I suggested.

I turned on the water and let it run for a few minutes to be sure it was nice and hot. Without first checking, I jumped in. *Bam!* The water was freezing. I came out of the shower screaming like a girl. We later discovered that the gas hadn't been turned on yet in our unit.

So Linda and I collapsed in the bed. We didn't kiss good-night; we just passed out from exhaustion. The next day we got the gas on in the apartment. We ended our short three-day honeymoon by sitting at home peacefully watching television.

There is a saying in the theater: "A bad dress rehearsal means a good show."

I would like to paraphrase that to say that a bad honeymoon can lead to a good marriage if you love each other.

We have now been married for more than forty years. Some years ago we were in Burger King ordering a sandwich. I began kidding Linda and she laughed. The more she laughed, the more I kidded her.

Soon the teenage girl behind the counter was also laughing.

"So it does work," she said.

"What's that?"

"Oh, you know. Love, marriage, and all that. I can see it in your faces. You love each other."

"Yeah, it does work if you let God be the center of it. And keep your sense of humor."

–C. Michael Bobbitt

~

From the very beginning of their marriage, Mike and Linda developed a high bounce-back factor. What's that? Bouncing back when your marriage experiences unexpected events. Recovering when things don't go as planned. If we have a highly successful bounce-back rate, we're able to cope without getting too upset or frustrated.

After all, challenges will happen. And when they do, if we get upset and allow ourselves to wallow in disappointment or frustration, it only makes our situation worse and our feelings more negative. And our marriage suffers.

Learning to take life in stride and developing an optimistic view— even laughing at the minor skirmishes—can help us grow individually, and closer together. Learn to have a bounce-back kind of love.

The Only Sure Foundation

I don't know if I can love you."

I will remember those words for the rest of my life. He was my boyfriend, my best friend, and the man of my dreams, but he couldn't love me. He couldn't love anyone.

"I want to marry you. I want to take care of you, and if we decide that we shouldn't have gotten married in the first place, we can always get a divorce," he said.

Four days later John and I called a business in the yellow pages, Anytime Weddings. They sent us to a minister's home in San Marcos, California, where we exchanged vows we didn't mean with people we didn't know, thus beginning our life together—on a foundation of broken glass. It wasn't long before that broken glass started to hurt and we were left wounded and bleeding.

For the next three years we found every possible way to hurt each other. Financial deception, adultery, and miscommunication burned through any trust we had for each other. Every time we tried to work things out, something happened to blow our momentarily happy life out of the water. We didn't always know what we were going to fight about, but there was always a fight.

Finally we decided to separate. It was over. It was going to take a miracle if our marriage was to survive the mess we had made of our lives.

"Are you sure this is what you want?" We had asked the same question the day we started this farce of a marriage.

Now, as we stood in the airport terminal saying good-bye, we asked it one more time. Tears streamed down both of our faces as I put luggage tags on the suitcases we had bought for our honeymoon. John pulled me to him. Tears flowed freely in our embrace, our lips met in a final good-bye.

"I will always love you," I said as I stepped toward security.

"I know." His blue eyes were rimmed in red. Blowing a kiss, he waved good-bye.

I stepped through the gate into a future I never planned. I always thought it would just work out, no matter what circumstances surrounded us when we got married.

I found my seat and collapsed into the tiny amount of personal space that would share my tears for the next three hours.

I landed in my parents' open arms. Ever supportive, they didn't say anything on the long drive from the airport to my childhood home. That changed when my bags were unloaded in the shelter of the bedroom I hadn't called mine since high school.

"You better get ready for church." My mom said it clearly enough that I knew I had no choice.

I hadn't been to church in years, and this was definitely not the time I wanted to hear people tell me how much God hates divorce or what a mess I was making of my life. Still, I would have to go. Skipping a service was not an option, even at twenty-seven.

Sitting in the pew next to my mother felt strange yet familiar. It was nice to see Daddy lead the congregation in prayer and announce the upcoming revival. Faith had always been such an important part of their lives. Almost thirty years into their marriage they still prayed and served together. I was jealous. I wanted that, but after less than four years my marriage was over. God certainly wouldn't want me with that kind of track record.

At first the service was fairly predictable. Three hymns, a praise chorus, the offering plate. But as the soloist began to sing a song about God letting us go to try our own wings, my tears came.

By the time she reached the chorus about God letting us go so we'd know we couldn't make it without Him, my face was saturated in salty tears.

I couldn't stand it anymore. I got up and walked to the back of the church. I had to get out. I pushed on the heavy door to the foyer and landed in my dad's arms. Together we walked to the altar.

As I stood bare before the Lord, I knew two things for sure: my life had to belong to the Lord, and my marriage had to have a do-over. I had to find a way back to John.

Six months later, armed with renewed faith, I went home. John was less than happy to see me, but he let me stay. I prayed every day for two years that God would save my marriage and draw John to knowing Christ. Eventually that day came. John gave his life to the Lord. We were going to make it. With Christ as the center of our marriage, there was nothing we couldn't get through.

"I never thought I could feel this much love," John told me on the way home from church. "I know for the first time in our lives that I love you."

He was grinning from ear to ear. Tears stung my eyes and I slid closer to him in the seat of the truck. Sitting close enough to feel his heartbeat, I was sure our troubles were behind us. I was wrong.

I grew up in the church. My dad was an evangelist. I had a foundation to build on even though I had turned my back on it for years. John's family, on the other hand, went to church on Sunday but never understood the need for a personal relationship with Jesus Christ. He had no foundation of Scripture in his heart. He wanted knowledge of biblical things. I wanted to get going on God's plan for our life.

When our pastor suggested a marriage retreat, we both scoffed. But we went, prepared to get nothing from the experience. As the weekend dragged on we became aware that this particular retreat was not for those who had been through trouble; most of our retreat mates were newly married or just looking for some time to reconnect. We retreated to our cabin in an effort to get *something* out of the money we spent to be there.

"Let's just have our own retreat," John said with a less-than-spiritual look in his eye, but I thought maybe he was on to something. I grabbed our Bibles from the dresser.

"Okay," I said, "let's open these randomly and take turns reading where they land."

He shook his head, sure I had not gotten his intended proposition, but he obliged anyway.

We spent the entire afternoon reading Scripture together. God's Word opened doors to conversations we had never had. We laughed, we cried, and we grew closer over random passages perfectly appointed by our heavenly Father.

That night we went to the evening service with a renewed confidence in God and in our marriage. The speaker talked about reading Scripture together. We smiled knowingly at each other as he suggested getting started by reading and discussing randomly chosen verses. But we listened intently at the suggestion that we should go further by studying together, praying for each other, and sitting quietly before God as a couple, listening together for His direction.

Returning home, we purposed to read together at least three days each week. Our household became one of peace and faith. Over the next several months we fell in love all over again—with each other and with the Lord.

In the summer of 1999, we renewed our wedding vows. I will remember his words for the rest of my life: "I love you; I always

have. I want to be with you for the rest of my life. I want to honor
God in our marriage and with our lives."

–PAMELA SONNENMOSER

~

One of the leaders in the Bible, Paul, encouraged people who were married to unbelievers not to leave their spouses if the spouses were willing for them to remain (1 Corinthians 7).

Being "unequally yoked," as the Bible puts it (2 Corinthians 6:14 KJV), or at different levels spiritually, is not good for a marriage, but when we're already in a marriage, as Pamela was, that's the reality we have to deal with. That's where the value of prayer comes in. As we pray and honor a spouse—no nagging or spiritual better-than-thou guilt trips!—God can do amazing things in that person's heart. If you're married to an unbeliever or a person who doesn't seem as interested in God as you are, don't give up hope. God is able to reach another person even when we think that it's just not humanly possible.

Money Can't Buy Me Love

I was twenty years old when I uttered, "Till death do us part."
I married Alton, my Prince Charming, and we rode into the sunset with empty pockets. My uncle poked a little fun at us when he remarked at my wedding reception, "This time you married for love—next time you'll marry for money."

His cynical words did not amuse me. Many people considered my husband and me an odd couple. To put it simply, we came from opposite sides of the tracks. I grew up on the upscale side of town with well-educated parents who had worked hard to provide me with the best of everything from a beautiful home and clothes to travel and vacations.

Alton was the son of deaf parents who had also worked hard to provide for their family. With no high school diplomas, their hard work barely garnished enough to pay their bills. As a result, my husband learned to work for what he wanted. Starting with a paper route, he developed a strong work ethic early in life.

Our marriage plans went against the grain of common sense and the materialism of the American culture. My father was the first to warn us of the difficulties this union could bring. He wanted his little princess to be well taken care of.

Some of our friends issued the same sentiment. My brother had married the heir to a family fortune. His wife told me, "Your marriage will never last—it just can't. You'll wake up and realize you've made a mistake. You two are just not of the same social strata."

Thanks for all the encouragement, I thought.

While dating Alton, I had also dated other guys in an effort to please my dad, who always told me to play the field. Many of those other guys were born into more material wealth than I was. But none of these suitors drew me like my handsome prince, whose humble background only enhanced his character. After dates with these others, I always fell back on, "But he's not Alton."

Could this marriage work? We thought so. Our spiritual hearts and goals in life were the same, and that compatibility was where we laid our case to rest. After five years of dating on and off, we believed we could face life together.

When we met with our minister, Dr. Scott, for premarital counseling, we asked him about the difference in our backgrounds. After all, everyone was concerned about it.

Dr. Scott gave us the secret to a successful marriage.

"A Christian marriage is like a triangle with the bride and groom at the bottom corners and God at the apex," he explained. "As we grow closer to God through prayer and Bible study, we grow closer to each other."

He also emphasized the importance of commitment to one another and spiritual compatibility. This is why the Bible clearly commanded us to not be tied together with unbelievers, he said. The Bible's admonition was not about money, it was about marrying someone who shares the most important part of life—one's faith.

Ours was an unusual wedding. The thousand who came to wish us well included senators, members of congress, and governors, as well as many poor and struggling people. We expressed our vows in voice and sign language. A wealthy entrepreneur told my father at the reception, "I have never been so impressed with true love as I have seen demonstrated in this couple today. If they ever divorce, please don't tell me; it will crush me."

Alton did not have enough money for an engagement ring. The ring would come three years later. But we were happy to be together living by faith. For the first ten years, both of us were students. We studied the Bible together at Columbia International University. Praying together was an integral part of our everyday life.

We graduated from CIU and continued at the University of South Carolina. I was eight months pregnant when I proudly walked across the stage to receive my graduate degree. When my husband received his doctorate, I handed him our three-year-old son and one-year-old twins for his cap-and-gown picture.

We survived one inch above the poverty level, yet we had all we needed and always had each other.

Our marriage grew and prospered through lean times. My father wondered how we paid the bills. He expected that we would need him to rescue us—but we did not.

There was no denying God provided for our needs. We graduated debt-free. When the twins were born, I was ready to settle down. We were finally able to build a home for our family and lead a more normal life. No one worked harder to make that happen than my Prince Charming.

And no one was a better father than my Alton. His job of running a residential school for deaf children took many hours, but he always found time for his wife and sons. We were finally living our fairy-tale dream.

Then my husband accepted a job as a professor at Clemson University. It was tough to put our house on the market and start over. Alton commuted the first year. When I was offered a job at a school in the Clemson area, my husband encouraged me to take it.

"But our house hasn't sold and we can't make it for long with two house payments," I insisted.

"Have faith, my dear. I feel you should take that job," he encouraged. "We've been praying about this for six months. I sense God telling me we should step out in faith."

With one son already in college and twins soon to enter, I did not feel this was the wise thing to do. I wanted to have faith, but I was the one who paid the bills.

Regardless, I signed that job contract and followed my husband's step of faith. During the summer, we moved to an apartment, leaving behind eighteen years of accumulated connections and relationships. I kept reminding myself to have faith.

Then came September 11, 2001. I watched as terrorists attacked our country and created a sense of fear. That fear told me our home would not sell anytime soon. We drove to our old city once each week to make sure our house was still showing well. Meanwhile, my father was diagnosed with Alzheimer's and I was spending weekends caring for him.

I would actually sleep in three different cities in one week. Some days I woke up not knowing where I was. My body was weary and my spirit was low. The two together brought me to a place I had never thought I could go—depression. I was beginning to understand why my uncle had made that cynical remark about marrying for money over love.

My husband had never seen me like this. He began to wonder if he had missed God's will and had made the wrong decision about moving. I made sure he took the blame for it. After all, I was angry he had put us in this position. If only he had brought money into our marriage, we would not be struggling.

I was only making the situation worse.

As each month passed with no resolution to our problem, I began to lose hope things would improve. My husband did everything he could to make it up to me. He massaged my feet to help me get up in the morning, and he held my hand tenderly as he prayed each day, "God, please sell our house!"

But the months of waiting and paying double housing expenses continued. We walked daily to keep my serotonin levels normal. And we prayed.

I was still struggling with depression when I attended a trustee reunion for our denomination's mission board. While there, I learned we were not the only ones caught in a move and burdened with a house that we couldn't sell.

"Times are tough," one pastor said. "You've just got to wait it out praying for God's grace."

I realized how much I had blamed my husband for everything. Instead of accepting his leadership, I questioned it. When I got home, I asked his forgiveness and we waded through the turbulent waters together. Finally, after thirty months of trying to sell our home and depleting our savings, it finally sold—the week before our twins entered college.

After we sold the house, I wondered if God was trying to teach me something. Why did He let the difficulties last so long? Perhaps He was reminding me what I knew all those years ago: What matters most in life is not what I have but the relationships I sustain with those I love the most.

The divorce rate in our country increases; unfaithfulness and finances stand out as two primary reasons. You can't turn on the TV without hearing about the infidelity of politicians and celebrities. Prenuptial agreements are normal for those who have riches. Yet no amount of money can guarantee the success of a marriage. Spiritual compatibility and drawing close to God are the superglue that holds a marriage together. In addition, commitment through good and tough times seals the marriage.

The richest things in life can't be bought with money. This year we celebrate our thirty-fifth wedding anniversary. Our marriage has survived cancer, depression, moving, financial crisis, college, children—including twins—and caring for and losing parents. My husband promised my father he would take care of me—and he has lived up to his oath.

The Beatles were right; money can't buy anyone love. Dr. Scott was right, too, when he told us money is not the glue that holds a marriage together. It's faith, commitment, loyalty, and unconditional love. And I'd marry my prince all over again. Not for money, but for love. I still believe in fairy tales where people love forever and grow old together as they ride into the sunset.

–GINNY DENT BRANT

How often do we fall into the trap of believing that our lives, including our marriages, would be so much better if only we had money?

While riches can certainly be a reward for hard work, and while it brings fun and blessing and the ability to bless others into a marriage, wealth is overrated. Money can also bring trials of its own.

Being in a marriage without excess money does bring some benefits. We may not be distracted by toys that would keep us from focusing on each other. And while it's not fun, surviving financial struggles together can draw us nearer to each other. Best of all, when we have needs, it can be fun to see how God meets them!

Perhaps the key, as Ginny has found and Paul has noted in the Bible, is to learn contentment whether we have plenty or are squeaking by (Philippians 4:11).

My Mentors in Caregiving

From our very first date, my wife, Glenda, instinctively knew how to care for my daily needs. I was a ministerial student. When I filled in one evening for a pastor at a midweek service, I invited Glenda to go with me.

As we returned to her dorm that evening just before curfew, her monster-sized ex-boyfriend, who played football at another college, appeared and growled at me, "I'm gonna kill you."

Glenda had to hurry into her dorm before the door locked, but hanging out the window of her second-floor room she shouted, "You hurt him and I'll never talk to you again!"

That gave me time to gingerly back up toward my car and slip away into the night—alive. By the next fall we had married.

For forty years we have cared for each other in our own ways, even though we sometimes didn't hold the traditional roles in our marriage and family. Because my wife has an accounting degree, I've left our money management to her. I come from a family where men cooked—my dad cooked for Kiwanis pancake breakfasts and banquets—so I cooked for most major holidays and when we had parties or guests.

Like many husbands, as our children grew up I worked long hours—fifty to sixty per week, sometimes more. For about twenty years I was a salesman, sales manager, and partner in a clothing business; for not quite twenty after that I was a pastor. My wife worked outside the home, too, as a medical business manager.

Glenda grew up in a home with a chronically ill mother. As a result, her caregiving skills developed early. But ten years ago, the week before Christmas, caregiving reached a completely new level even for her.

The ranger at the park near our house found me lying unconscious on a lakeside road where I often biked for eight hilly miles three or four days a week. My bicycle was lying twenty feet away.

I was rushed to the city's best trauma center, where I was diagnosed with a closed head brain injury. After three days in a coma, I spent three weeks not recognizing Glenda, family members, or concerned friends. I awoke to discover I would need to walk with a walker and therapists would need to retrain me to walk, feed and bathe myself, and perform other basic tasks of self-care. I learned that Glenda had slept on a cot beside my bed all but one night since I was hospitalized. That continued until I was released.

For nearly two years after that, I appeared to be permanently disabled, mentally as well as physically. In spite of months of speech therapy I spoke with a slur, struggled to find words, and often used the wrong words. During that time Glenda took over. I remember her buying me expensive items I would never have bought for myself, such as fancy padded tennis shoes.

She also took me on a trip we had fantasized about going on in retirement. We flew to Los Angeles, rented a car, and drove up the West Coast to Seattle. We followed Highways 1 and 101, skirting as close to the Pacific Ocean as possible. For three beautiful weeks we visited such places as Carmel-by-the-Sea on the Monterey Peninsula and Astoria, Washington, before flying home to Kansas City.

During those two years I gradually recovered and began wondering, *How can we afford this?*

We were comfortable but not rich. Glenda had always managed our money well. The only time we'd bounced a check was forty years earlier when I'd written it. We never even had an overdue bill payment.

But still I wondered, *What's going on?*

When we returned from our trip, I began to notice how often Glenda needed to sleep. I noticed that now before board meetings she had to make notes about financial matters of the groups she managed. In the past years she could recall from memory the previous year's expenses and that year's budgeted amounts. I had assumed she needed the notes because she was working with larger medical practices, but maybe that wasn't the reason.

Then tax time came. Normally Glenda had filed our taxes well before the deadline. That year she had to file for an extension, and even then, she struggled to finish our return. In the following months she began saying, "You'll have to start helping with this" and "You need to learn to pay our bills."

I stalled. I'd never done our taxes or even balanced our checkbook. She was the accountant, not me.

Because so many odd things seemed to be going on, we took Glenda to see a neurologist, who diagnosed her with vascular dementia. How was that possible? She was only in her mid-fifties.

In addition to the dementia, she developed a severe hearing loss. In spite of her two digital hearing aids, I had to repeat things over and over.

She responded with "Use your preaching voice." But when I raised my voice she often interpreted that as anger. Although I wanted to deny it, sometimes it was frustrating. Even when she heard my words, her dementia often hindered her ability to understand them.

When Glenda responded with anger or tears, I felt guilty and wondered what a caring response should be. Gradually I realized that the model to follow was the care I had received from her while recovering from my brain injury. I had been trying to think of caring things to do for her. One day I realized caring isn't performing what seems caring to me, but accepting her as she is and doing what she feels comfortable doing.

She enjoys walking our two Yorkies, so we walk a couple times a day. We even bought little coats for them so we don't have to stop in cold weather. Like many dementia patients, Glenda is confused by change and new situations, so I don't suggest taking trips anymore or going to places that aren't familiar for her.

I love what's left of the person I married almost fifty years ago. I'm thankful for Glenda's basic personality, which is positive, good humored, and outgoing. Unlike many people with dementia, she isn't consumed with anger at her shrinking mental faculty. She laughs at one of her frequent comments, "That's the best meal I've had," or she might say it's the best episode of a TV program she enjoys. The joke is it's the only meal or the only episode she can remember.

What the future holds I can't predict. The neurologist told me a few years back that Glenda will need a nursing home in five to ten years, but that hasn't happened yet.

Whatever comes, I'll follow my neighbor's good example for providing care when worse comes to worst. His wife has Parkinson's disease. Her condition degenerated until she was bedridden. She can't move unless helped from bed into a wheelchair and then pushed to where she wants or needs to go. He's past ninety and no longer is able to safely help her. Consequently, she had to enter a nearby care center.

Each day he goes to the care center, sits by her bed, and reads the newspaper. At lunch he helps her into her wheelchair and rolls her to the dining room, where they eat a meal with another couple. He's still devoted after all those years.

In caring for Glenda I try to follow her example of patient caring for me after my accident. My neighbor's actions serve as a guide for preparing for what may lie ahead. Perhaps in the coming years I'll be a role model for other caregivers.

–JIM RAWDON

*G*row old with me; the best is yet to be," poet Robert Browning wrote. Sometimes life sends us unexpected curveballs. And for some couples, growing old has more challenges than for others.

As Jim found, when we love, we learn to do whatever we need to do to take care of the one who is precious to us. When we love, it's amazing what resources we find from within us, around us, and from the Father. Though the thought of caring for someone to a serious extent may look scary, as Browning also says, our times are in God's hands. Even amid turmoil and illness, who knows? The best days of marriage may still be ahead even after decades have passed.

Where's the Bread?

My husband has no internal dialogue. He verbalizes every thought that pops into his head, no matter how trivial.

Case in point. When David makes a sandwich, he walks into the kitchen and says, "Where's the bread?"

Now, for years that question launched me into a major attitude zone because I assumed "Where's the bread?" was his way of saying, "I don't really want to make my own sandwich so I'm going to bug you until you make it for me."

The first few years of our marriage, his sandwich making looked like this:

David: "Where's the bread?"

Me (not very patiently): "The bread is right where you left it the last time you made a sandwich. It's called a *bread box.*"

David (undaunted): "Where's the mayonnaise?"

At that point I gritted my teeth and fished mayo out of the fridge, thrusting it in David's direction.

David: "Where's the salami?"

You get the picture. By the time he got to, "Where's the speckled mustard? Where are the pickles? Where's the lettuce and tomato?" I'd chase him out of the kitchen and slap the sandwich together while he wandered off with, "Where'd I leave my drink?"

I just assumed men were clueless. Then one day I was having lunch with my sister, who was complaining about a houseguest who'd overstayed her welcome.

"I swear, the woman has NO internal dialogue!" my sister exclaimed.

No internal dialogue? What the heck did that mean? Then she described this friend looking for a pair of shoes: "Now, where'd I leave those red shoes? I wore them to the art opening Wednesday night, came in, and got ready for dinner. I could have sworn I left them . . ."

That's David! I thought. All those years when I assumed he was trying to shirk his duties when he asked, "Where's the Swiss cheese?" he was only *looking* for the cheese.

Hmmm. I thought about the way he plays cards: "Six . . . seven . . . eight . . . darn . . . no nine." The way he surfs channels: "ESPN . . . Discovery . . . why do we need twenty-four-hour weather?" And the way he finds a listing in the phonebook: "A . . . B . . . C . . ."

No internal dialogue. That's it! Now I had a diagnosis. I watched him that night preparing his baked potato at the dinner table. "Sour cream, little salt, dab more butter." *Absolutely no internal dialogue.*

I watched him change the oil in my car. This was particularly funny because he was outside and I was watching him through the window so I couldn't see his face or hear what he was saying. But I could see his legs jutting out from under my car and our old collie wagging his entire body with excitement because—of course—he assumed David was talking to him. In dog language, "Dang, how'd

I get this thing off last time?" sounds a lot like, "Good ol' boy, wanna go for a walk?"

Clearly the dog loved the whole lack of internal dialogue.

So does our three-year-old. Since he's at an age where he jabbers from sunrise to sunset, it's nice for him to have someone to talk with—if not to. I watched the two of them this morning as David attempted to pry up some weeds that had crept through the cracks in our front walk. Jonah was talking on about alligators, sharks, and bears while David pondered, "You'd think these boogers would just come right up. How deep do these roots go?" They both looked pretty content.

A friend called this morning to gripe about how she and her husband never talk anymore. David was next to me changing the batteries in one of the kids' toys.

"He comes through the door at night and I'm lucky if he says two words before he walks back out the next morning," my friend complained.

"Where's the Phillips-head screw driver?" (This from You-Know-Who.)

"When we were first married, we talked for hours; now I barely remember what his voice sounds like."

"I had it when I was working on the screen door. When was that?"

"Last week I decided not to speak to him and see how long it took him to realize. Two days went by and he never even *noticed*."

"How does this darn thing open?"

"I found a book about reviving the communication in your marriage. I'm halfway through it, but I don't know . . ."

"Counter clockwise. Counter clockwise."

"The big question is, can I convince him to read it?"

"Plus. Minus. Plus. Minus."

"So do you ever have problems like that with David? I mean, y'all have been married for twenty years. Does David still talk?"

"Where'd that dang screw roll? I need that screw."

"David? Talk? Oh yeah, David talks. He definitely talks."

"Ah, there it is. Now, how do you switch this thing on?"

—MIMI KNIGHT

⌒

S ay *what you mean and mean what you say." The old adage can cer- tainly be true in marriage. How many times do we read the wrong message into the words—or actions—of our mates? Sometimes our assumptions are totally off base. Like Mimi, sometimes we need to stop and say, "Are you just processing your thoughts verbally, or are you try- ing to get me to do something without directly asking? What exactly do you mean by saying (or doing) this?"*

Asking for clarification can help us keep from getting upset with- out cause. And it can even help us know our mates better—giving us intriguing new insights into the distinctive conglomeration of personal- ity traits, thoughts, and experiences that create the essence of the person we love!

$\mathcal{L}$ove on the Rocks

"No pain. No gain." It was a fine motto for some, but not one I particularly lived by.

Through my early twenties, I'd established a well-tread pattern of exerting myself just to the point where things became really difficult. And honestly I'd done okay. Why would I pursue the hard way when I had achieved relative success with little discomfort?

Then I met my husband, Dan. From our first date I was hooked. As we got to know each other better, I noticed Dan was different from others I'd dated. He was driven—from the inside. Not in a financial-gain kind of way, but in a succeeding-over-adversity kind of way. He climbed mountains, ran marathons, and completed triathlons.

I was intrigued that ordinary people could do stuff like that. And I wondered if somewhere in me existed that kind of gumption.

When Dan suggested we go backpacking for a weekend in the Catskills, it seemed like a fun thing to try. After college I'd traveled through Europe with a backpack and Eurail pass; I figured this would be basically the same—but with more wildlife and fewer overly attentive Italian men.

We planned our trip, filled our packs, and set out to climb a mountain. My adrenaline flowed as we hit the trailhead and said good-bye to the car for the weekend. What fun and adventure lay ahead!

Do you know that hiking up a mountain with a loaded backpack is hard? Really hard. Like, *Okay, I've had enough, let's go back to the car* hard.

After a few hours, sweat dripped from my brow, the pack dug into my shoulders, and my boots hurt my feet. This was not what I'd signed up for. *No, sir.*

I was tired and frustrated. Tears burned my eyes as I stopped to free myself from the behemoth on my back. I found respite on a nearby rock and waited for the love of my life to notice the absence of my huffing and puffing behind him. I knew he'd rescue me from this cruel place and whisk me to somewhere more comfortable.

Instead, Dan—who is a quitting-isn't-an-option kind of person— returned to where I sat. He sat next to me, put his arm around my shoulder, and looked me in the eye. Then he tapped my chin with his fist and uttered words that live in infamy in our relationship: "Aw, buck up, little camper!"

My head swirled. Was I so fatigued I'd become delusional?

"Buck up"?! Where was his sympathy? Where was, *"You're right sweetie, let's go back to the car"?*

This was not the response I'd expected at all. It wasn't fair! I was tempted to storm off in a huff, angry I wasn't coddled, as I'd hoped. But I didn't. In fact, I couldn't. Dan had the map, the compass, and the car keys.

It was the kind of moment that makes or breaks a relationship. I could have stormed away from this insensitive ogre, or I could begrudgingly follow and see what happened.

While I wasn't particularly happy, I brushed off my wounded feelings, gathered my inner resources, and continued hiking—all the way to the top, where we set up camp, enjoyed great hiking, and marveled at the spectacular views from the summit.

On the mountain that weekend I learned some valuable lessons.

First, I can handle far more than I ever imagined. Second, there really can be victory on the other side of pain. Third, sometimes I need a good, strong nudge to keep going.

At the time I had no idea how much I'd need to revisit these lessons in the future.

Shortly after our backpacking weekend, Dan and I married. The adventurous yet intimate bond we shared while dating carried into our marriage. We set up house, got a puppy, and continued our adventures together. While some of our newly married friends struggled to work out the kinks of full-time togetherness, Dan and I felt our honeymoon lasted for years. I didn't work hard at our marriage because I honestly didn't have to. Sure we had disagreements, but somehow we quickly found our center and worked things out.

In time baby made three, and a few years later, four. With a daughter, a son, and a golden retriever, we were a typical all-American family. We lived a blessed life.

As a stay-at-home mom, I shifted focus from my husband to our children. Marriage took a backseat to the ever-present needs of little ones. I spent the early years of motherhood like a triage nurse attending to those requiring the most care and attention.

"What about me?" Dan occasionally asked. I had little to offer but a few meager scraps of affection and attention.

Our children grew and weekend adventures were replaced with school concerts, carpools, and Saturdays on the sidelines of soccer, basketball, and football games. Dan and I still carved out time for occasional dates and weekends away, but our day-to-day reality centered on keeping aloft the parental balls we juggled. Our marriage wasn't troubled, but the emotional intimacy that marked our beginning years was replaced with a divide-and-conquer mentality.

Then seven years ago Dan started his own business. Even though this meant the loss of benefits and a steady income, I supported his decision and was thrilled he was finally taking a chance to use his God-given talents.

Dan pursued self-employment with the same intensity he had

when hiking. Failure was not an option. He worked long and hard. Shortly after he started, one of his clients asked him to be a key player in a huge project. This type of assignment usually went to those who'd worked in the industry for years—not someone just starting out.

We celebrated the opportunity. That is, I celebrated until I learned what the project entailed.

"It's a nine-week product launch in Canada," he said.

Having no experience with these sorts of things, I asked, "So, you'll come home on the weekends, right?"

"Not exactly," he replied.

It turned out Dan would come home for only one week the entire time. My joy vanished and I ranted, much as I had on a mountainside years earlier, "This is unfair! This isn't what I signed up for! Tell them you can't do it. How am I supposed to be a mother *and* a father?"

But no amount of pouting or complaining altered his plans.

Dan went to Canada as scheduled and, much to my surprise, I didn't crumble. The kids and I settled into a routine and did okay on our own. Thus began a new climb in our marriage and life as a family.

In the ensuing years we endured lots of days apart and more long-term assignments.

I "bucked up" as best I could, and with each trip I got better at managing the house and caring for the children on my own. In fact, we used a few of the trips as mini-vacations. Twice I traveled alone to visit Dan on location, and once the kids and I flew to California during another job.

Unfortunately, travel wasn't the only issue. Far from it. Even when he wasn't away, Dan worked such long hours it seemed he rarely emerged from his home office. Yet as trying as his schedule was, I remained proud of his accomplishments. He was respected professionally, he loved his work, and he excelled at what he did. And he made enough money to support our household.

I knew the long hours and travel schedule came with the territory, and since Dan was the primary breadwinner, I tried my best to remain supportive. With each large project that came his way, I'd tell myself, *Okay, just press on through this one. When it's over it'll get better.*

Except for an occasional breather, that break never came. One assignment led to the next. One deadline gave way to another. As the years passed, my patience wore thin. I often prayed for strength and understanding, but I grew tired of continually explaining Dan's absences to our friends and family—"He's in Atlanta." "He has to finish a big job this weekend." "Oh, Dan's in the U.K." I fatigued from carrying so much of the parenting load on my own.

Worst of all, instead of struggling to adjust to my husband's absence, I found it harder and harder to adjust to his *presence.* I was getting too good at traveling solo.

Finding grace for a workaholic husband was hard. After seven years, I reached my limit. I felt crippled by years of unspoken resentments and marital neglect, and distanced by the emotional walls we'd erected for self-protection.

Where was the fun? The adventure? The togetherness? I'd tried my best to soldier on, but when I gazed at the path ahead I saw a never-ending uphill climb that led to more of the same. I couldn't imagine my marriage or our family life continuing on this way.

Quitting would have been the easy answer. Many marriages end over lesser struggles. But if I learned one thing from Dan over the years, it was that giving up wasn't an option. I still believed in our marriage, and Dan did, too. Plus, we hadn't just promised each other " 'Til death do us part." We'd promised God. So, frustrated and unhappy, I confronted Dan. "That's it! I've had enough. I can't live like this anymore!"

Ironically, it seemed our blind perseverance was the reason we'd gotten so off-track, and it took things getting that bad for us to really face where we were—and where we were headed. Thankfully this time, when I plopped down discouraged and disillusioned, Dan didn't "comfort" me with the kind of trailside pep talk he had two

decades earlier. Instead, this time he said the very words I most
needed to hear—"You're right." It seemed he, too, had learned
some lessons on this hike.

It was another turning point in our relationship.

We came together and set down the burdens we both carried.
Dan shared something I hadn't considered: Even though he'd experienced years of success while working on his own, he still feared
failing his business and ultimately his family. To counteract this,
he'd kept pressing on intensely through each job, rarely saying no
to his clients. The phone kept ringing and new work kept coming
in. But Dan was just as frustrated as I was that each successfully
reached deadline turned out to be another false summit. He, too,
was looking for respite and wondered if he was even climbing the
right mountain.

It would have been handy if we could've pulled out a marriage
trail guide to show us the way to go. But once my husband and I
started to honestly communicate, I found that we really weren't far
apart after all. We still shared the same values, hopes, and dreams for
the future. So we returned to the basics that had carried us through
our backpacking adventures and all the years of our marriage—
teamwork and shared goals. We started to lay out a new map for
our future.

First, Dan addressed his work schedule. Both of us wanted him
to continue his business, but we agreed Dan needed to find ways
to control his schedule so it didn't control him—even if it meant
making less money. He started to delegate and outsource, and even
say no once in a while. I've found there are ways I can pitch in and
help him out from time to time that offer relief and make me feel
part of the team. It's a work in progress, but for the first time in a
long time, we feel like we're in it together.

Second, I recommitted myself to bucking up—not by my own
strength, but by God's. Ecclesiastes says, "A cord of three strands is
not [easily] broken" (4:12 NIV). As I got frustrated with Dan over the
years, I'd emotionally and mentally checked out. I avoided putting in

the hard work necessary to keep my marriage on track—but I forgot I didn't have to do it all on my own. Years ago God answered my specific prayers and miraculously changed my heart when it came to accepting Dan's travel schedule. In the ensuing years I'd gotten away from praying for my marriage and my husband. More than anything I needed to resume an active prayer life, and to not change Dan but change myself.

Finally Dan and I are starting to rediscover the very thing that brought us together in the first place—fun and adventure. Even if it's just lunch together, a long walk, or a romantic dinner. It's almost like meeting each other all over again. We're also getting our kids involved in our outdoor ventures, where we've created some of our best family memories.

This spring marks our twentieth wedding anniversary. Recently we discussed options for celebrating it in style. At first we visited the obvious choices—a romantic bed and breakfast retreat, a beach weekend in Bermuda, maybe even a short cruise. As we rejected one idea after another, an obvious answer emerged. Last week we placed our deposit on a four-day backpacking trip from the North Rim to the South Rim of the Grand Canyon.

We'll continue our adventure right where it began. With love . . . on the rocks.

—KELLI REGAN

The movies make it look so easy. If two people are meant for each other, then everything will go smoothly. Problems melt away easily. Cultural wisdom tells us if a couple's romance is laden with difficulties or boredom, maybe the reason is because they're not supposed to be together in the first place—and they should move on to someone new.

While we can hope for smooth sailing and work toward having a carefree life, it's generally true that nothing good in life comes easily.

And just because something is difficult doesn't mean it's bad or not where we should be in life.

As Kelli found out, while we may not welcome pain, as we persevere through it, it can still bring gain to marriage.

Sometimes, Just Say No

Tears streamed down my cheeks as I drove to work. The angry exchange of words with my husband from the night before echoed in my head.

"Why did you do that?" Loren asked. "We agreed we weren't going to give him any more money."

"But he said he needed gas to go to work until payday." I reasoned. "And he promised to pay it back on Friday."

Angry, Loren shook his head. "How many times has he borrowed, promised to pay, and never followed through?"

I knew my husband was right, but how could I say no to our eighteen-year-old son? Wouldn't that drive him further away?

Most likely he ran short on money because he spent it on any number of poor choices that had defined his life during the past two years. He had led us on a journey into the dark world of drugs and gang activity. It was a world we knew nothing about. We were in shock, and neither of us knew how to respond. Loren thought I was too soft, and I thought he was too harsh.

Twenty years of a predominately happy marriage and now it seemed our whole life revolved around the choices our son was making. We couldn't agree on anything. I knew I loved Loren, but sometimes I felt like there was nothing left.

I pulled into work and sat in the car as I dried my face and struggled to regain my composure. I was exhausted; we both were.

This is not how I want to live. I just can't take this anymore, I thought.

Our son's behavior had pitted us against each other. I was sick of the almost daily arguments. Sleep deprived and in constant turmoil, I had come to the point where I didn't even want to go home at night. That was the moment I decided to check out of my marriage. That evening I would stay with my parents. Loren and I needed a break from each other anyway, I rationalized.

I walked into work to face the retail public. My heart hung heavy throughout the day, but only God and I knew the lie behind my smile as I waited on customers. Finally the last shopper left. I locked the door and dimmed the lights. I stood at the counter closing the day's books when the owner's wife came in the back door.

"How are you doing, Kathy?" she asked.

She knew about the situation with our son and had prayed for me many times during the past two years. With a questioning smile she searched my eyes. My heart split open and the pain gushed forth. When I had finished, she offered some wise words of advice.

"You're married to Loren, not your son. That's the relationship you committed to, and when the kids leave home, that's the one that needs to stand." And she added, "I know you love Loren, and he could never live without you."

I thanked her as we gave each other a hug.

"I'll finish up here. You go on home," she told me.

Somewhat relieved of the day's stress, I left the store. When I opened the door of my car, a huge bouquet of flowers rested on the seat. The attached note read: "Kathy, I love you and I don't want anything to ever come between us, not even one of our children. We can work through this. I'll see you at home. Love, Loren."

That evening Loren and I had an honest talk. We recognized we had to cling tighter to each other and focus on the Lord and our faith in Him. And we needed a plan in order to survive the chaos.

We made an active choice to stop letting our son's lifestyle run our lives. That meant saying no when he called for money, even if it meant leaving him in jail instead of bailing him out. From that time on, whenever he asked for a loan I directed him to his dad. And I trusted Loren to make the right decision.

Then we knelt beside our bed and prayed for each other. Weeping before the Lord, we prayed for agreement between us and for strength and wisdom in the days ahead. We also prayed for our son and released him into the Father's care. It was evident to us that only the Lord had the power to rescue him.

As soon as we could arrange it, Loren and I took a trip to the Oregon coast, our favorite vacation spot. Getting away helped us rest, refocus, and reconnect. Once refreshed, we would be better able to deal with the crisis that bombarded us daily.

When we came home we continued to pray together every day. Whether it was in the morning before work or at night before bed, we made prayer a priority. We asked for greater understanding of each other in what we were going through. We prayed for the Lord's wisdom in our responses to our son. And we prayed for strength to say no: no to those who tried to put extra demands on us, and no to our son when he tried to manipulate and involve us in his poor choices.

While our son continued his destructive path, we worked to preserve our marriage. Our family continued to face challenges throughout this six-year ordeal. The constant strain on our emotions drained our energy, so we reenergized by going to bed early and getting the rest we needed.

I'm thankful we persevered through those years. Our son

eventually emerged from the fog bank he was in and is rebuilding his life. What a tragedy it would have been if we had let those turbulent years destroy our marriage. We realized the best thing we could do through this pain was to remain faithful to each other.

–KATHLEEN KOHLER

*O*ne of the biggest pressures in a marriage can be when a child brings extra stress and the parents don't agree on how to handle it. It's easy to focus on a child's problems so much that we lose sight of each other. Kathleen's boss had wise words. Although our children mean the world to us, a marriage commitment is made to last long after the children are gone and pursuing their own lives. Though our kids' choices can break our hearts, we can't let their choices ruin our relationship with each other.

While parenting can be demanding, a wise couple takes—and makes—opportunities to be together, to focus on each other, and even to "ban" talking about the children and domestic problems for the evening. Commit your children to God, who is better able to create change in their lives than you are! Then let yourselves forget about the children and concentrate again on each other. Sounds impossible, but it really can work!

The Irresistible Orange Coat

And it came to pass in those days, that there went out a decree from Caesar Augustus that all the world should be taxed" (Luke 2:1 KJV).

Well, one good thing came out of our unexpected tax bill. Ron and I had a faint glimmer of what Mary and Joseph felt like when they heard that news. Taxes! We were newlyweds, barely making ends meet from week to week.

Then we got the tax bill.

Maybe the whole world wasn't in a tax quandary, but our little township municipal staff suddenly decided to change the time of billing. We had two months to save two hundred dollars out of nothing. That would take some doing, for sure. And it was Christmas, too, the time of year when we would be obligated to spend more money.

We started by cutting back a little on our food. That wasn't too painful. We had a freezer full of beef and vegetables, but I stopped buying so much sugar, coffee, and other nonessentials.

I had looked forward to carrying on my mom's holiday baking traditions in my own home. No sugar meant that I couldn't make and decorate Mom's sugar cookies, her triple-fudge brownies, or even her famous maple nut fudge.

I made the family's Christmas gifts out of what we had around the house. I wasn't much of a knitter, but I attempted socks for my brother. Unfortunately my tension was a little off. They would have fit Paul Bunyan or Andrè the Giant. My teenage sister was not interested in a crocheted doily. My dad was trying to quit smoking so he didn't appreciate the ashtray!

Need I go on? Let's just say you would have preferred not to get a gift from us that year!

We didn't even buy antifreeze for our twelve-year-old truck. Instead, Ron drove it right up to the edge of the house every night, drained the radiator, and covered the hood with an old quilt. The muffler needed replacing, but we thought we could put that off till after the dreaded tax bill.

That meant constant noise and a few fumes. We conquered the fumes by driving with the windows slightly ajar. Whew! The noise was another issue. Neighbors knew our schedule by heart. They greeted us with words like, "I heard you leave yesterday morning. Got an early start, didja?"

Ron had to take a part-time job off the farm. That meant the cow and I were left together. And I said hello to the old pregnant sow on a regular basis. It meant Tilley, our horse, and I seeing eye to eye a couple times a day.

I knew all about farm life. I am a born and bred country girl. Why, I'd even belonged to 4-H calf clubs at my father's insistence! However, I never intended to make a career out of being close to animals. Ron's family sheltered their gals from farm work, and believe me, I liked it that way. Now with Ron working, I shoveled interesting product, lugged grain pails, and stirred slop. Yippee!

We scrimped and saved our way to January 15, the looming tax deadline day. Ron and I carefully counted the small pile of currency we had gathered. We had just enough. Ron went off to his job, relaxed in the notion that all our hard work had paid off. The responsibility of visiting the township office and paying the taxes fell on me.

Unfortunately, Hill's Department Store was between that municipal building and me. And it had the biggest sale signs in the windows! I hadn't been anywhere to just look around, not in so long, and my friend Jean was driving; I really had no choice, right?

When she suggested we just stop for a moment, I succumbed. As Jean said, the money was safe in my handbag. What could happen to it? The sale looked great. The municipal building was on the other side of town, after all. We could go there later.

What would it hurt to just try on a few things? I mean, didn't I deserve a feminine moment or two? After all, for our first Christmas together, my hubby presented me with a roasting pan!

Yes, of course, it was a wise gift. The old one leaked. I needed a new one. It was cheap. We had no money and it cost about three dollars. Still, it wasn't a very romantic thing, now, was it?

So if I just lightened my heart a little by trying on a few things, well, what could it hurt? And . . . well you can see where this is headed, can't you? We went in.

It was a madhouse. Surely every woman for thirty miles around jammed the building. They battled each other over racks of dresses and shelves of hats. They paraded new shoes before mirrors and stuffed lacy underwear into their shopping baskets.

And then there was me, cowering in a corner with my handbag squeezed tightly under my arm. I followed Jean to the coatrack, simply because I didn't want to be alone with all that cash. While Jean stuffed herself into coat after coat, I only watched and nodded a yes or no to each one. After a few minutes of this, Jean tired of looking for things to cover her body. She turned her expertise to mine.

I put my bag down carefully between my feet and tried on a

number of coats. I told myself that I was just being a good friend. Honestly, I only did it to please her!

And then, somehow I was leaving the store with a full bag under my arm; however, it wasn't my handbag. No, *that* was quite empty. You see, Jean had found me the perfect coat. It sounds garish now, but then it was the height of style. Orange and brown threads formed a tweed pattern. It had a fitted waistband topped with a leather belt. The final selling point for me was the wonderful fur collar.

No. That's not true. The final selling point was Jean, whispering into my ear, "Oh, that coat is absolutely perfect for you. And it's half price. Where will you ever find another bargain like that?"

Later, I thought about an old comedy skit in which a woman tried to explain to her hubby why she spent so much on an outfit. The lines went something like this:

Hubby: "Why didn't you just say, 'Get behind me, Satan'?"

Wife: "I did. He said the dress looked great back there, too!"

I found myself outside the store with the coat, an empty handbag, the tax bill, and a crowing Jean. "Oh, Brenda, you got such a deal! Aren't you delighted? Let's celebrate your good luck. I'll treat. Let's go out for lunch."

And she did treat. I let her. Why not? She still had all her cash.

I was broke and nearly sick to my stomach. I forced my sandwich down, all the time I wondered how on earth I could explain my foolishness to my sweet, trusting husband. You might wonder why I just didn't take the coat back. I couldn't. All sales were final, with no refunds.

What if I just told the truth? Yikes! I knew what I'd do if he'd bought tools or something instead of paying that bill. I would yell and never let him handle our finances again.

I stewed all afternoon. I thought about how I would tell Ron. I dreaded his return from work. Somehow that coat didn't look nearly as bright and wonderful and cozy now. Now it just cried out "guilt!" I stuffed it in the closet. I didn't want to see it ever again. It made me nauseous to look at it.

I thought about trying to resell it, but I didn't know anyone who would be foolish enough to buy it! After all, even though it suited me, at first glance, it was orange! Who on earth would be stupid enough to buy an orange coat? *Sigh.*

I decided to soften the blow by preparing Ron's favorite meal. Flavorful beef stew with lots of meat, potatoes, and carrots simmered on the stove. I'd add dumpling batter at the last minute. An apple crisp browned in the oven. I polished the house from top to bottom—and waited.

Ron arrived home right on the dot of six. I put on my bravest smile and met him at the door. He kissed me. We made small talk and then he asked the dreaded question. "Did you pay the taxes today?"

I felt as if he'd punched me in the stomach. For a moment, in spite of my afternoon of practiced answers, I was speechless.

I started to cry. "Oh, honey, I did an awful thing today. I spent the tax money."

Ron didn't say a word. He simply waited.

"Oh, honey, Jean wanted to go to Hill's sale and before I knew it, I'd bought a coat. She said it looked great on me. And it really does. Do you want to see it?"

I waited. Nothing happened. Ron didn't yell or throw things or stamp his feet or anything. He just looked at me.

I don't know how to explain that look. So many years later it continues to haunt me. His face was full of disappointment, sadness, hurt, and discouragement. Yet through it all, love shone and melted me.

The shame I'd felt was nothing compared to the complete knowledge that I'd let my honey down. We'd scrimped and saved for two months, and all for nothing. We still owed taxes, but now we'd have to pay interest. Ron would have to keep that part-time job. The animals and I would become special long-time friends. All because I had to have the coat.

The rest of the evening passed uneventfully. The stew was a

success. The dumplings turned out as light as a feather. The apple crisp tasted scrumptious. The small talk continued. The undercurrent of silence remained deafening.

Of course, we eventually gathered enough money to pay the taxes and the interest. I learned to make better financial choices. Our lives moved forward. We had children. We paid for our farm. We became more financially sound. Years passed. Still, I remembered that look and I wore the coat for every occasion. How could I not? I felt so guilty about the whole episode. Every time I wore that coat, I felt shamed.

About ten years later, I noticed how the coat's fur collar had frayed. Broken belt loops betrayed their age. Snags covered the fabric. The coat was done for. I could finally throw it out with a clear conscience.

First, though, I asked Ron what he thought about my getting a new coat. I showed him how battered the orange one had become.

"Honey," he said, "I didn't notice that. Why have you waited so long to buy another coat?"

I confessed my long-held guilt.

"Sweetheart!" he cried. "I forgave you the minute it happened. I never thought of it again. Why did you?"

Finally I understood what real forgiveness looks like. Ron had given me the gift of forgetfulness. My coat decision hurt him in so many ways, but still he forgave it. Then he forgot it. Not once in all those years had he ever mentioned it to me again.

And I learned, too, that bygones are meant to be bygones. In our marriage we learn from our mistakes, and together we leave them in the past. No argument or "hot discussion," as we call it, ever contains a throwback comment from something we did many years ago.

By the way, I still use that Christmas roasting pan. It didn't wear out like the coat. It reminds me of how our love grew through hard times. It's a symbol that guilt is best let go, especially in the face of forgiveness.

—BRENDA WOOD

~

While most of us will not be buying orange coats, we will make mistakes—sometimes so outrageous and huge we can't believe we've done it! It's hard to confess our sins and errors to our spouses. And sometimes we're way tougher on ourselves than they would ever be. Communication is a key in situations like this. And admitting, "I'm really mad at myself for doing this. Are you as mad with me as I am?" And so many times we find out they aren't. Then it's time to release the guilt—to forgive ourselves and realize the one we love has, too. To look our beloved in the face again, shamelessly forgiven, and not let our mistakes hinder the relationship.

Managing Pain Together

When the phone call all parents fear reached my ears on a beautiful spring night in 2002, there was no way my wife and I could have foreseen the challenges that would lie ahead.

First we'd received a mild alarm from our seventeen-year-old daughter's close friend Katie, who called and said, "We think Melissa's been in a car accident."

A few anxious minutes later, a more frantic call came from another friend. Then a scream into the phone, which was followed by the shocked voice of the mom of one of Melissa's classmates, who verified the awful truth: "Dave, I'm so sorry. I'm so very sorry. The police will be coming to your home."

Our youngest daughter would not be coming home that night—or ever again. Melissa was in the passenger seat when her friend made a driving error. She was taken from us on the last day of her junior year in high school.

I turned from the phone call that night and looked at my precious family—our son, Steve; our second of three daughters, Julie; and my wife, Sue—to mouth those horrendous words: "Melissa's gone."

Sue collapsed into my arms and sobbed over and over. "The pain is too great to bear. The pain is too great to bear."

And so it is. The pain for parents who lose a child suddenly and prematurely is indeed more than a human can stand. It is sometimes more than the most ardent faith can support. And it is often more than a marriage can withstand.

As Sue and I began our sad new life that night—the life of grieving parents who have just seen our dream family shattered, our precious daughter taken, our future hopes dashed into splinters of hopelessness—we did not know anything about how a child's death affects grieving parents. We just knew life would never be the same for any of us. And we knew that somehow we would have to face each new day hobbled and in despair.

We stood for ten hours by Melissa's side on visitation day as hundreds of well-wishers temporarily and graciously buoyed our spirits. And after we said an aching graveside good-bye to our daughter under appropriately gray skies, the truly hard part began. We muddled along from day to day after Melissa died, beginning to see the ways such searing grief could pull apart two people who are deeply in love.

We had been married thirty years and had faced numerous challenges, as all couples do. But we would need help. We would need all of the spiritual resources we had gained from a lifetime of trusting God and attempting to shine Jesus' light on the world. We would need to understand each other in new ways as we began to work through our rearranged lives.

Most important, we would have to accept the different ways spouses grieve.

Sure there were similarities. We both were brought to tears by anything that reminded us of Melissa's death. We were less interested in some of life's peripheral things such as entertainment and sports. Laughter didn't come as easily. And we both had little use for canned Christian advice about how to process this hairpin turn of events in our lives.

We both searched what we knew of God's Word to try to make some sense out of seeing our beautiful, godly daughter snatched away—while all around us we saw other young people throw their lives away on things we were sure God detested. We both were angered with parents flippantly joking about being glad to have an empty nest or how happy they were when their kids went to college. Those sentiments accented how much we wished we could have just five more minutes with a daughter who would never graduate from high school or go to college.

But while the similarities abounded, so did the differences. And those differences were major challenges to the new "normal" we had to accept. Our differences were lessons for us in how a couple can survive while not seeing everything the same way. They were exercises in understanding and love.

For instance, Sue could no longer attend the church where our family had served and worshiped for twelve years. But I continued to attend and drag Steve along. For Sue, walking through those doors would have been like turning on a video loop of missing memories—of sitting proudly with our kids and worshiping. Being there without Melissa would have only added to her searing pain.

Therefore, for two years, we seldom worshiped together—and that is never a good situation. I would take Steve to our old church to try to give him stability, while Sue would worship at a megachurch so she could have anonymity and escape from tear-inducing memories.

Sue could not force herself to return to our kids' Christian school, which we had been associated with for more than twenty-five years. On the other hand, I longed to be more involved there. I wanted to be around Melissa's friends and other high school students because they reminded me of her and her love for life; Sue could not stand to be around them for the very same reason. To me, the reminders brought joy. To her, the reminders brought nothing but more cracks in a broken heart.

While I worked with the teens at Melissa's high school and even traveled with them on overseas ministry trips, Sue was left out of the loop. My enjoyment was tempered by Sue's confusion as to how I could be around these kids. This caused added tension in our marriage, for it was another activity we could not share. While I was with the kids, Sue was left alone in her grief.

In Steve's schooling and church, he felt more like his mom.

How could we force him to go to this school every day and be reminded of Melissa, he argued. How could he walk through those doors and not see his big sister in the hallways laughing with her friends, he wondered. Why were we forcing him to go there when he wanted to be anywhere but there, he protested.

Our family had been our life. We had raised each of our children—Lisa, Julie, Melissa, and Steve—to love Jesus Christ and to serve Him. Our lives revolved around the Christian world—the kids' involvement with Children's Bible Hour, our integration in the church scene, their attendance and participation at their Christian school, my job at Radio Bible Class Ministries, Sue's job at a Christian nursing home.

And yet life turned into a daily battle over God's role. About whether to trust Him again. About how to keep our son—who was angry with God for taking his best friend, his confidante, his sister—from running away from Him. About how to keep him in a school where we knew he had advocates and friends who would keep a spiritual eye on him. About how grieving parents taking different routes could still travel through life together.

Tensions grew. We made mistakes as Sue and I tried to keep our relationship strong while parenting a grieving son. As Steve grew more bitter and estranged from the Christian life, Sue and I were often at odds about how to deal with him. Should we let him go to the public school, knowing he often gravitated toward the roughest crowd? How much space should we give him as he tested our standards and values?

Steve was a different person; but then, we were different, too.

Sometimes the pain was too great to let us be the parents we had been for his sisters. Sometimes the pain got in the way of the caring, loving relationship Sue and I had carefully nurtured.

Steve suddenly went from the little brother of three adoring sisters to the only child still at home with grieving parents. We didn't know him. And we didn't even know each other as well anymore. We often didn't know how to continue.

Melissa's death also affected our finances. Besides not being able to attend our church or visit our school, Sue couldn't work at her old job. Melissa had worked there part time as a kitchen aide while Sue was an in-charge nurse. The pain of returning to a place she shared with Melissa, and the lack of energy caused by grief, meant she could not return. For two years, Sue could not work anywhere because the pain was so great.

Meanwhile, we decided to move from the home in which we had raised all four kids, to a more secluded one that was more conducive to the quiet we needed for grieving.

Yet this is when the financial impact of having just one breadwinner slammed us the hardest. While we loved the new home, it needed a ton of work. So I rolled up my sleeves, hauled out my credit card, and got busy.

When we finally moved in several months later, I had put tens of thousands of dollars we didn't have into our grief house. And despite the sale of our old home, we started out life in our new place with some heavy debts.

I say "we," but I should say "I." In an attempt to protect Sue, I had not told her that we were living off the sale from our previous house, and I did not put as much of that money into paying off our new home—something we had agreed to do. Plus, I had huge credit card debt hanging over my head.

Not knowing what to do, I tried juggling payments and bills—always getting further behind and never telling my soul mate what I was doing. Eventually, Sue figured out the mess we were in.

Grieving parents face trials almost too numerous to detail. But throwing financial irresponsibility into the mix, I discovered, is a backbreaker. Sue was hurt that I hadn't told her, and upset that we were in a battle for our financial lives.

After many weeks of tension, after the expenditure of some carefully protected life savings, and after Sue's considerable forgiveness, this crisis was finally put to rest, and life returned to a new normal.

We learned lessons about open communication, about not letting circumstances get in the way of good decision making, and about not throwing away our faith in God because of our despair.

Grieving parents suffer pain long after a child has been laid to rest. Every day some residual hurt rises to snatch joy from a mom and dad's heart. Few weeks pass without a painful memory sneaking into life—forcing parents to deal with their differences, to feel the pain, to seek solace again from each other's depleting reserves. Year melts into year, but the aching never stops. The similarities never overcome the differences. The sunshine never shines as brightly again.

Only as we have accepted God's sovereignty in this situation, only as we have allowed each other the freedom to feel and express pain, and only as we have accepted the fact that we are not the people we used to be—whether in personality, emotion, spirituality, energy, or focus—have we been able to cross the valley of the shadow of Melissa's death. Only as we learn to have the courage to trust God again and as we find help from the fact that Melissa's story is helping others, have we been able to hang on to life.

Yes, the pain is too great to bear. But we've learned if we can survive this pain together and still love each other as much as ever—we know that God still has some great things in store for us as a couple.

—DAVE BRANON

*S*tatistics are high on the breakup of marriages that have endured the loss of a child. Any point of grief can cause stress and changes that put pressure on the marriage. As Dave learned, each person expresses sorrow and lives through grief differently. And while people in a marriage are a couple, the two individuals may be going through very different emotional and spiritual experiences. What may bring comfort to one may bring pain to another.

Through the severe grief points in marriage, sometimes we have to accept that we may not really understand exactly what our loved one is feeling—and that's okay. Though energy is at a low, striving to communicate is a key—even a simple "I know I seemed harsh; it's just grief talking."

Couples going through the heartbreaks of life can survive the storms—but it takes lots of grace and lots of forgiveness. Remember that while grief will totally change our lives, better days will eventually come. Hold out for those better days.

$\mathcal{A}$ Little Romance
Goes a Long Way

O n the morning of our eleventh wedding anniversary, we exchanged the usual, "Happy anniversary, honey."

At that, Jeff jumped out of bed. "Got to get to work!"

I lay back on the bed. My head sunk into the pillow as I reminisced over our eleven years together. I pondered how much my love for my husband had grown over those years. A smile crossed my face as I thought about our dating season and how persistently he had pursued me. He won my affections with his romantic notions and gentle, easygoing way.

I thought about our plans and dreams. I was even seeing some of them come true. Jeff and I both enjoyed creativity. In fact, he was a sign painter and an artist. I admired his diligent, hardworking spirit as he succeeded in building his own business, and I supported him unquestioningly. I even tolerated the long hours and the weekends he worked without complaint.

"I'll do anything to help my man succeed," I determined. I thought that's what a good wife should do.

Just as I tolerated Jeff's drive to succeed, I felt he accepted the fact that I was dealing with a chronic illness that restricted some of my activities. Although neither one of us liked it, we managed to get through without much complaint.

Our love for each other appeared unconditional. There was no pretense about it. I never had to pretend to be someone or something that I wasn't. He accepted me just as I was and I him. I was grateful for that.

As our anniversary day progressed, it wasn't much different from any other. We didn't have an exchange of cards with loving sentiments. No trip to the theater or dinner date. Part of my illness involved environmental sensitivities, so I had become housebound.

Over the years Jeff and I had our own way of sharing special moments, such as eating a bowl of popcorn in front of a romantic movie. It satisfied us, as far as I could tell.

Not long after our anniversary passed, I noticed a change in my husband's moods and affection. I couldn't quite pinpoint the problem, but he seemed indifferent when I approached him.

I was concerned when he started becoming short-tempered with me. Each day he would call me on his breaks from work or trips to the supermarket. Now his phone calls weren't so frequent. And when he did call, the conversation was brief. I felt a distance was building between us.

One day as I was looking out my front window, I caught a glance of a young woman walking down the street. The way her hair glimmered in the sunlight caught my attention. I noticed her bright red lipstick and colorful clothing. I glanced at my wedding photo on top of the table. I looked at how my hair shined and makeup highlighted my facial features.

Fixing my hair and putting on makeup were part of my everyday regime back then. That had changed when I became chronically ill. I tended to wear a cotton dress every day and no makeup. My dull, dark hair included strands of gray. I longed to be that vibrant woman again. Nothing was sensuous or appealing about this old gal.

I leaned back in my chair and squeezed my eyelids to keep the tears from streaming down my face. I heard that still, small voice well up from inside of me, "You need some romance in your marriage."

I pondered what the Lord was telling me. He was right. We needed some spice in our relationship.

As I swayed back and forth in my rocker, my eyes rested on a wicker basket in the corner that I'd received at my bridal shower. For years it sat there with some of my sentimental books in it—including a book on tips to romancing your mate. *I bought that book when Jeff and I were newlyweds*, I thought.

I'd tried a few of the suggestions back then. But as sickness took its toll, the book remained untouched for years.

Jeff romanced me, but now I only romance my illness, I thought. *I need to make an effort to romance him in return.*

I picked up the book and spent the afternoon going through it, noting which ideas I thought could work for us.

God seemed to place some other ideas on my mind. I'd avoided makeup for years because of an allergy to the chemicals. But now He seemed to prompt me, "You can buy makeup made of new minerals now. . . . Try some of that."

I got on the Internet and picked out some basics. When the packages arrived a few days later, I hurried to the mirror to try my new treasures. I transformed right before my eyes. *Wow! I look so much younger and better . . . just like my old self.*

And as the weeks passed, I was thrilled not to have any sensitivity reactions. *This is good!*

Next, the Lord reminded me of the way Jeff wooed me when we were dating and newly wed. In the beginning of our marriage, Jeff had always written notes to me. I'd open the car door and get into my seat and notice his words of love stuck to the steering wheel. He gave me cards for every imaginable occasion. He had been attentive, too. He'd packed my lunch for work and cooked me special meals.

I put pen to paper and started writing love notes, leaving them in various places around the house. I found a box of old cards Jeff had given me. I rummaged through the box. The sentiments stirred the passion in my heart and I started recycling them back to him.

I found one old card in which Jeff had thanked me for a rose and mentioned that no one had ever given him flowers before. Maybe it was time to try that again. A friend picked up a red rose for me and brought it by.

That night when I climbed into bed, I placed the fragrant red rose on his pillowcase.

When he came to bed, he caught a glimpse of the bright red flower.

"Who gave me this?" he asked with surprise.

"I did," I replied.

"Thank you," he said quietly.

I fell asleep that night thinking that the ice might be breaking. But the next morning, the distance returned.

Like a dedicated soldier, I stayed the course. One day I decided to look through my closet for new attire. I found a bright blue blouse that glittered, and slipped it over my head.

"WOW! You look great in that color!" Jeff exclaimed when he walked in the door that night.

I held on to every glimmer of hope—I was fighting for my life and my marriage. Some days brought more tears and frustration than encouragement. But when I took a close look at what was happening, I noticed a new life emerging in me. As I was romancing my husband, God was healing me.

One day in my prayer time God prodded me to start going out of the house. "You've been in so long now; try strengthening your immunity to the environment."

This was a huge fear for me to conquer. Going outside had always caused my sensitivities to act up and I'd become ill. I hesitated, but I decided I wanted to try to overcome them, so I walked in my driveway a few minutes each day, speaking Scriptures pertaining to healing and marriage.

My next outside adventure was to try to tolerate car rides. So I'd have Jeff take me for rides to the nearby beach. Since the lake was romantic, besides stretching me, I thought this might ignite a little romantic passion.

Besides outward attractiveness, God spoke to me to be kind, loving, and compassionate. As I was willing to make changes, God was helping me make progress.

It took time, but within the next year Jeff started to notice me again. He surprised me with compliments.

One day Jeff came home from work and asked me to go to a restaurant with him. This was a huge struggle for me, considering how the smells of some spices affected me. As I sat across the table from Jeff, I noticed butterflies in my stomach.

As we talked and laughed, Jeff asked, "Have you noticed this is a date?"

Slowly but surely our love began to grow again. Jeff started coming in from his workshop earlier each night, and we began spending quality time together each weekend.

I watched in awe as our relationship blossomed! As a result, we grew closer to the kids and were growing into the healthy, happy family that I'd always dreamed of being.

God was true to His promise. He was giving Jeff and me a new beginning and reviving my life! Each day I work toward my physical healing and discover new ways to romance my spouse. After all, it's fun!

—ANNETTEE BUDZBAN

⁓

*H*ow can I love thee; let me count the ways." That modification from Elizabeth Barrett Browning's famous poem should permanently become part of our lives. It's natural for the romance in a marriage to slow down. After all, if we always put the energy into our relationship now that we put into it before marriage, it would be nearly impossible to get anything done.

But everyone longs for a little romance in his or her life. When Annettee began to look for ways to remind her husband of her love, she found them—and a lot of the tips to romancing her spouse were as near as remembering how she looked and behaved back in the early days of courtship.

Sometimes the relationship has grown so cold or unemotional that it's like romancing a stone—or at least a stone heart. But as we're persistent, we can make cracks in the hardest exterior.

What are you doing to romance your spouse today?

God Does the Altering

The most romantic day of my life was when I walked down the aisle in our little church toward my Prince Charming, Larry, who waited for me at the altar. I couldn't wait to become his wife. God had brought us together, and since our marriage was made in heaven, I just knew it would be perfect.

Even though I believed Larry was God's perfect gift for me, I had an underlying philosophy of "I'll get him to the altar and then I'll alter him."

Larry was certainly wonderful, but a few rough edges needed some work. After all, I was God's perfect gift for him, too—to help him become all God wanted him to be.

On that magical day, Larry's Prince Charming armor shined as it reflected the candlelight at the altar. Let the marriage begin!

And in the beginning, it was all fun and games. I loved Larry's take-charge personality. He was confident and made quick decisions.

I, on the other hand, was more cautious about life and wouldn't make a decision until I had analyzed every part of the situation.

But as our first year came and went, the very things I'd liked about Larry when we had been courting became sources of irritation. His take-charge personality seemed to cover every area of _my_ life. One day he told me, "Kathy, you should put the drinking glasses in the cupboard with the rim down. That's the way my mother does it!"

_Oh?_ I tried to let the criticism roll off my back.

Within a few days, Larry commented, "Kathy, you put the toilet tissue on the wrong way. It should be facing the back rather than the front. And did I already mention that you aren't squeezing the toothpaste tube at the end? Don't squeeze it in the middle."

"I guess I just can't do anything right," I muttered, but Larry seemed unaware of my unhappiness.

And my plan to alter him was frustratingly ineffective. When he criticized others, I tried to point out how being compassionate inspired people to change. My wisdom fell on deaf ears. Although I felt irritated, I was hopeful that in time I could inspire him to have a more gracious perspective.

But by the time we'd been married seven years, my Prince Charming's armor didn't just have some spots—I saw gaping, rusting holes. The hopelessness and helplessness had been building for two years.

At our anniversary dinner out on the town I unwisely asked again, "Larry, why do you work so many hours? Why can't you help me at home more? Having a two-year-old and a newborn is such hard work; I need you to help me."

I immediately saw his sour mood gush into self-protection. "Kathy, I've tried to help you see that I'm working all these hours to secure our financial future."

Silence again surrounded us like a dense fog at the beach. And then another fog, the fog of hopelessness, encircled me again. _Kathy, you never do anything right! He must really hate you!_

In my own defense I mentally screamed, *I hate him, too!*

The next day, the tension from the night before continued to bother me. Doubts and fears haunted me: *Will we get a divorce? Why can't we talk? We used to be so in love.*

And just as quickly, I prayed, "Lord, we're Christians; we're not supposed to be acting like this. What's wrong?"

My altering project was rusting just as much as Larry's armor. Larry worked two jobs and had a flying hobby. He was a policeman, sold real estate, and rented a plane almost every week to fly his friends somewhere.

One Saturday he announced that he would be gone flying for the day.

I quickly spoke up. "Honey, we haven't had family time together for so long. I'll get the kids ready and we'll join you."

"Kathy, I only rented a two-seater plane and I already asked Joe to go with me. You just stay home and have a nice, quiet day with the kids."

I could sense the frustration rise inside me. *A quiet day with a two-year-old and a newborn?!* Who was he kidding? I needed to get out, not stay home!

He turned and walked down the hall that led to the laundry room and into the garage. As I followed him, trying to think of words that would make him stay home, my anger built. When he closed the laundry room door behind him, my fury flared. It was as if he had slammed the door in my face, showing me how unworthy I was of any love.

I remembered the apple I was eating and threw it. The apple shattered against the door, sending little red and white pieces all over the small room, adhering to the walls. The apple core fell to the floor. I stomped into my bedroom, knelt by my bed, and inwardly screamed, *God, make his plane crash! I don't care if I ever see him again!*

After I'd calmed down, I picked up the apple core but I didn't wipe the apple pieces off the walls. Over the following months, those rotting apple pieces became my memorial to our rotten marriage. I concluded, *God, you can't put those apple pieces back together. Neither can this marriage be put back together.*

I wasn't even sure I wanted it healed. My heart had grown cold and bitter.

The more hardened my heart became, the more I was determined to make Larry aware of my unhappiness. When he was home, I nagged him. I made snide comments about how little attention he gave the kids. My daily grumbling rolled around in my brain. *When Larry becomes the good husband I need, I'll become the happy and contented wife he wants. It's all his fault we're at odds. If only he would change, I would, too.*

Then one day as I did my housework, I sensed God's gentle words in my heart. "Tell Larry you love him."

Whoa! Where did that come from? Love him? You've got to be kidding, God. I don't love him; I hate him. And if I tell him I love him, he'll think I approve of everything he does. I won't say it because it's not true!

I tried to concentrate on my work, but God's command interrupted me again. "Tell Larry you love him."

No! I was adamant. *He's away on another flying trip and didn't take me again. I'm not about to give him ammunition to use against me.*

I expected that would silence Him, but again I sensed God speaking. This time the message changed slightly. "Then think it the next time you see Larry."

Think it? What good would that do? He won't even hear me!

Oh! He won't hear me. Okay, I mused, *then he can't use it against me.*

I paused and then reluctantly agreed. "Okay, God, I do want to be your obedient servant."

For the next several hours, I told myself over and over again, "I'm going to do it. I'm going to do it, even though it's not true."

That evening when I heard Larry enter the house, I knew he was walking through the laundry room where the rotting apple pieces still decorated the walls. He walked down the hall toward me. I told myself, "I'm going to do it," gulped, and hesitantly thought, *I love you* . . . and after a pause, added, *but I don't really.*

In that moment there was a shift in my thinking. It was tiny, but even that small choice buried a godly seed that over time began to grow. I had made a disgruntled decision to love, but I realized I could do it again and again, in obedience to God.

The more I made that choice, the more the Lord did surgery on my heart. For the first time I took responsibility for my own ungodly choices. I could recognize that God could empower me to change even if Larry never changed. In fact, Larry didn't hold the key to my happiness; God did. What if Larry never changed? What if I never could alter him? I would be unhappy the rest of my life, and that would mean Larry was inadvertently controlling me.

Could God really be enough for me? I decided He could. Even if Larry never changed, I didn't have to be discontented. The Holy Spirit wanted to empower me for joy and contentment.

"Okay, God, I surrender," I prayed. "Make me who you want me to be. I can't change Larry; I can only change myself. He's your project, not mine. You're better at the altering business than I am. I can't be Larry's Holy Spirit. Only you can. I give him to you and I give you myself."

Within minutes, I walked into the laundry room with my pail of soapy water and washed the rotting apple pieces off the walls and ceiling. I murmured, "I no longer need a memorial to my rotten marriage. It's in your hands now, Lord."

When Larry came home that evening, I had fixed dinner and straightened the house. I greeted him with a smile and a kiss and didn't complain that he was late. Over several months, I prayed constantly for God's help, and in time it became easier and easier to be cheerful. Even loving.

Larry would tell me later that he noticed. He didn't know what had happened, but he noticed. He wondered whether it would last.

I was actually shocked to see my change of attitude. I would have never thought it possible.

In time, Larry seemed to respond. And when he got a job at a different police department but had to take a cut in pay, he didn't have as much money to fly. He wasn't gone as much.

I couldn't believe it. God had changed the circumstances in His timing and in His creative way. All my nagging and complaining had never made Larry stay home; it had only driven him away. God worked in a way I never could have devised.

Little by little, our relationship strengthened. I fell back in love with my husband and again appreciated the strengths I'd loved in the beginning. He didn't need to be altered by me. My attitude did. And God changed his heart also to fall back in love with me.

Now we feel like we couldn't be happier or more in love, and yet every day it seems we are. What's almost as amazing is how we have each influenced, but not demanded, the other to become more of who God wants us to be. Larry has become more compassionate toward others because of God's transforming work. And I've become more confident knowing that God is truly in control of my life.

I'm so glad I made that decision to love and released the expectation that I could do what only the Holy Spirit can do. Only God can truly alter a human heart.

–KATHY COLLARD MILLER

In some cases the stereotype is true—people get married with the idea of changing the one they walk down the aisle with. And they find that the more they try to change the other person, the less it works!

Instead, we can make greater strides by offering each other the acceptance we long for in our own lives. And we can realize that sometimes a husband or wife is the way he or she is because God made him or her that way. If the person truly changed the way we wanted him or her to,

*it might destroy the essence of who that person is and eliminate the very
personality that drew us to him or her in the first place!*

*What's the old adage? If both of you are exactly alike, one of you
is unnecessary. Our marriages are strengthened as we learn to acknowledge, accept, and even celebrate our differences. Husbands and wives are
just intrinsically, in many ways, different. And as the French say,* vive
la différence.

Prayer That Leads to Wisdom

My husband came home from work one evening and, with a cold and indifferent tone not at all typical of him, frowned and cleared his throat. "Let's go for a ride; we need to talk."

His demeanor, somber and aloof, puzzled me.

I threw on my bright red sweater and off-white corduroy pants. I don't know why, but details of the clothing I wear in moments of intense emotion are vividly engraved in the depths of my memory. I rushed to comb my hair and joined him as he silently walked me to the car.

He opened the door and I slipped into the passenger's seat. Clueless about what he wanted to talk about, I clicked on my seat belt. He started the engine and we left our neighborhood without any specific destination. I guessed he had bad news. Did he lose his job? Did something happen to a family member?

As an uncomfortable silence accompanied us in the car, my hands grew sweaty and my stomach tight. "What's wrong?"

He drew in a long breath and spat words that seared my soul. "I'm not happy. I've wanted to tell you this for a long time." I held my breath. "There's another person in my life." His tone was sad and indifferent. "She works with me and I've been confiding in her."

"I don't feel well," I muttered.

That cold black bucket seat suddenly felt like an electric chair, sending burning bolts through me. His feeble explanations and justifications eluded me. I could only envision our three little boys and myself being added to the countless homes without fathers.

As weeks swept by, my house was no longer a home but a rubble destroyed by blows of bitter fights and fierce winds of sulky blame.

Alone and angry, I sunk deeper into the sand of sorrow while negative voices tormented my thoughts. I'd grown up with healthy notions of what marriage should be, but now I was confused and angry. I'd had no warning, no hint of his discontentment.

I'd been satisfied with my life, which up to then had followed a nearly perfect path. The news jolted me and brought a helpless feeling that burned inside.

How did it happen? When and where did I go wrong? Those questions rumbled in my head.

"God, this is not fair. Show me what to do," I cried during the sleepless nights. But I found no answers.

Then a dim light flickered through the fog and I saw a new revelation shine through: I had expected my husband to fill my deepest emotional needs—my security, my sense of worth, and my hope for happiness. I had looked to him as my provider of all.

He was supposed to be my partner, not my God. He was my companion, not the ruler of my emotions. He was my friend, not the source of my happiness.

With a clear view of my new path, my anger and self-pity turned to constant prayer for my husband. Renewed security in God fluttered through my heart. Instead of tormenting thoughts, sleep came back at night and calmness filled my days. Adding to my peace, understanding of God's definition of marriage gave me more clarity and focus.

With renewed strength, courage, and confidence, I addressed the issue once again. But this time, rather than a confrontation, I vowed it would be a peaceful dialogue.

"I didn't force you to marry me," I said with outward calmness, "and I won't force you to stay, either." My heart thumped. "God will be the Father our sons might not have, and He'll be the husband who'll never leave me."

Gene didn't respond. But days later he came home and asked if we could talk. He clasped my hand tightly.

"I made a decision." He said with conviction in his voice. "I will continue with our marriage."

Though my heart did a cartwheel, I remained silent. I'd learned that emotions should not guide my reactions. Rather, wisdom and confidence had to rule my responses. So I told him we needed to make a drastic change—we needed to pray together.

He hugged me and whispered, "Okay."

Then it was my turn. I sighed and braced myself to jump the toughest hurdle—to forgive him. After constant prayer I could take the leap and express complete forgiveness.

At first our prayer times were uncomfortable; they were quick and awkward. But we forged on. Our prayers expanded into genuine pleas for guidance. Then, requests for our marriage, our sons, and our needs filled each night's prayers.

Like the seasons, changes blossomed. I saw the spring of a fresh and healthier awareness of what I needed and who would provide it. The summer brought warm affection and renewed passion. The inevitable setbacks in life accompanied our fall but somehow painted a new color to our closeness. Winter then ushered more profound changes to our relationship, resulting in triumph over the coldness of tough moments.

Now our marriage has become a dance: I learned the steps, listened to the melody of love and forgiveness, and stepped onto the dance floor with confidence and trust. The music of life plays on and the rhythm echoes in my heart, reaffirming my decision to silence negative emotions and listen closely to the song of sound wisdom.

–JANET PEREZ ECKLES

*O*ne of the key elements to a successful marriage is certainly prayer! Sometimes when marriage gets to the stage Janet's reached we cannot do anything to save our marriage or change our mate except to pray.

Prayer is the seam that keeps our marriage from unraveling. Part of being a good mate is praying for the one we love so dearly. And praying together is like using an epoxy resin on our marriage. Something about prayer keeps us adhered tightly, even when pressures are applied. Praying together helps us learn what is on each other's hearts. As we pray together, two people become a team. As we come together before God's throne, we truly learn to be in tune with each other.

Beware of Barracudas on Bikes

Four years ago my husband and I had the incredible opportunity to venture to Austria on a two-week bike tour.

As soon as he told me about the trip, my heart sank. We had two young daughters and I feared leaving them for so long. Once I snapped out of my maternal delusion, however, I breathed a wonderful sigh of gratitude. This would be our getaway, our perfect expedition where we'd be enamored with Austrian sights and pummeled with overwhelming feelings of romance for one another again—two toddlers had a way of draining the romance from our five-year union.

I let my visions of our impending trip run wild. I dreamed we would dance in fields of sunflowers and fantasized that we'd have dozens of pictures taken by old relics. I imagined us talking all night, until exhausted from conversation we'd fall asleep in each other's arms.

The mind is a wonderful place for building unrealistic expectations.

And now for reality.

The trip is one of my favorite experiences with Steve. This is true. But it did not unfold exactly how I imagined it would. Pedaling our bikes for hours each day was exhausting. We didn't have the time I expected to take in the hundreds of views I had imagined. We did stop at antiquated churches, old pubs, and historical sites, but most views came at us as we flew on our bikes down hills or whipped around back roads.

On the other hand, the scent of pine needles, combined with the pleasure of being outdoors with my husband, paralleled no experience we'd ever had. I loved it!

We weren't the only bikers in our tour group. Four other couples and a single man and woman accompanied us. We'll call the woman Maria, though she was a far cry from the character in *The Sound of Music*.

Early in the trip we acclimated to the time change, the jet lag, and the Wiener schnitzel for lunch as opposed to the light lunches we were used to in America. Things seemed to be moving along smoothly, despite our bike-seat-blistering blues. The other couples were friendly and good conversationalists. But then there was Maria.

How was I to solve a problem like Maria? Let's just say she seemed a little too fond of the way my husband rode his bike. And she wasn't shy about expressing her fondness. As minor flirtation turned to more solid advances, I began to feel Maria was all that really stood between me and some of my romantic dreams for our trip. She was public enemy number one.

Steve and I discussed our discomfort with how she behaved around him. He shrugged off most of her compliments and made a point not to sit near her or engage in conversation with her.

But Miss Maria was relentless. She had no qualms about throwing a suggestive compliment my husband's way as I stood next to him.

By the end of week one, Steve and I strategized. We put a game plan together. We might as well have been entering a ball field, the way we talked through the whole awkward situation. We agreed to how we'd sit at meals, how we'd dodge questions, and how we'd stick together like Velcro.

To make matters a little more complicated, remember Mr. Single Guy? About the same time Maria was moving in for the kill, Mr. Single Guy ramped up his friendliness toward me. I'm a pretty straightforward person and had no problems being blunt with Mr. Single Guy, plus I doted on my husband whenever he came around.

The plot thickens, of course. You didn't think this would end right now with me and my husband dancing in fields of sunflowers, did you?

Only a few days remained of the trip. Steve and I managed to share wonderfully meaningful moments despite the inappropriate attention we were getting from the singles on the trip. Those moments would seal into the beautiful memories I still have of our bike tour in Austria.

But one day had the potential to ruin it all—at least in my mind. Our guide had scheduled a day of rest. By this time we'd entered Italy, and the women planned to shop in the village. The men decided they'd spend our "rest" day biking twelve miles to a nearby lake. I thought everything had fallen into place brilliantly. I'd get a shopping day. My husband would get a day to go be with the men and do man things.

I awoke, stretched my arms, and took my time getting out of bed. Steve was already gone. I bathed, dressed, and found the other women mingling on the cobblestone street.

As we started to talk, I went into shock. Did I just hear what I thought I had? Maria wasn't going to join us. Maria had gone with the men to the lake.

My heart flopped into my stomach. Maria was with the men. All day. At a lake. I pictured her prancing around at the water's edge in a bikini.

I shopped for twenty minutes. Then I hid in my room and cried for hours. Why had Maria spoiled the day for the men? Why had I let her ruffle my feathers? Why did she seem most attracted to my man? Tears didn't dissipate my feelings. But prayer helped, as well as the reminder that I trusted my husband. He had always proven himself trustworthy in the past.

After crying my eyeballs dry, I met with the ladies again and we discussed the strange turn of events. I revealed my insecurities and they encouraged me. None of us understood it, but we couldn't do anything to change what had happened or what Maria was doing, so we shopped and enjoyed the rest of the day.

Then the men returned. At the first chance, I got my husband alone. He said Maria's last-minute decision to join the men was awkward. He explained that she'd gone off on her own after they got to the lake. As I looked in his eyes, the pit inside my stomach dissolved. This was my man—my reliable, loyal, loving man.

That night at dinner Maria made a point to tell me how fast my husband rides on his bike. Then, oddly, the conversation landed on the topic of trust.

Maria looked at me and joked, "You trust me?" She dared me with her mocking grin.

Being the truthful person I am, I said, "No. No, Maria. I don't trust you."

We didn't have more problems from Maria for the duration of the trip. I eliminated public enemy number one but watched as she predictably moved in on another married man.

Eventually I think I have come to understand why Maria acted the way she did. I think Maria wanted what we had. She craved the solid connection my husband and I shared—the long, lingering looks and private jokes. We had it—and we still have it. Because we held on to it. We protected it. And we stood by the game plan.

–WENDY MILLER

*P*redators happen. Many people in this world do not respect the boundaries of marriage—and can even feel a challenge or thrill to try to climb over the fence of someone else's "property."

One of the keys to dealing with predators is to not be naïve. Just because we would never pursue someone else's spouse doesn't mean someone else holds those same morals. When predators lurk, we can be up-front about it with our spouse—perhaps your mate hasn't noticed the wolf stalking him or her. And conversely, when a spouse senses red flags, we can respect his or her perception.

Together, by acknowledging the situation and thinking ahead, we can make plans of action to deal with someone trying to encroach on our marriage territory. And ultimately, when we see predators stalking, we have to leave the situation in God's hand and trust our spouse.

Some Swan Song!

A parishioner poked her head into our church meeting room. "Your husband's in the parking lot—emergency," she said, her voice taut.

I bolted from my seat. When I reached our car, my stomach roiled at the sight of our five-year-old daughter's limp body in my husband's arms.

"Gotta get her to the hospital."

Bob handed Meggie to me, careful not to disturb the blood-soaked washcloth covering her forehead.

Fourteen stitches and two hours later, I tucked our kindergartner into bed. It wasn't quite as easy to tuck away the guilt I felt for not being there when the neighbor boy threw a board at Meggie. Still, I am thankful I didn't hear him yell "Bull's-eye!" as it tore into her head.

I suppose that should have been my first clue that I spent too much time away from home working on this committee or another. I wasn't there for emergencies or for evenings of family together time because of my "commitments." The years rolled by, taking with them endless hours of my away-from-home time. Our daughters grew and graduated from high school.

If the warning signs flashed along the way, I remained oblivious— I didn't see our marriage sliding toward the ditch. I didn't have time to notice. Not with working full time, volunteering for this and that, and doing what I did best—my own thing.

Granted, all these fell into the category of "woman" things—as my Bob called them. Nonetheless, my activities didn't include my husband. Why should they? He was off hunting and fishing and doing "man" things.

Surely he was as happy and content as I was. Why wouldn't he be? I kept a clean house, cooked delicious meals, refilled his underwear drawer with laundered skivvies every Saturday, and I stayed in relatively good shape. After almost twenty years of married life, what more could he want?

I'd invited him to join me in attending concerts, Valentine's dinners, parties given by my co-workers, evening walks, and rousing games of Pictionary or Scrabble. Since he consistently declined, I quit asking. He asked me to join him hunting. I begged off, content with my outside interests.

When we reached that twentieth anniversary, Bob presented me with a small gift-wrapped package.

"Happy anniversary," he said.

My first thought was, *I didn't get him anything.*

Shaking off a mental shrug, I peeled away bits of tape and set aside the wrapping. Lifting the box lid, I gasped with surprise. A stunning jade teardrop necklace nestled in the container. In the middle of the alabaster-colored stone, two gold swans swam side by side.

"This is the closest to geese I could find," Bob said before explaining. "Where the gander goes, the goose follows." He paused. "I'd like us to be like that. Together more."

My chest and throat tightened. I fought back tears, pushed to the brink by regrets and shame. I knew my husband wasn't saying he wanted me to follow him blindly, or for me to be subservient, but to join him as a mate—because he loved me and wanted us to enjoy things together.

My husband's message was the most defining moment in our marriage. At that instant, I resolved to reestablish my priorities. That was on October 16—hunting season.

A couple of days later I told him, "I want to hunt with you this year."

Bob's face brightened, and as he is a man of few words, he said nothing more about the subject.

A few days later he announced, "I'm taking you to Portland. Gonna get you something."

All right! That dress I've been wanting, I thought. Already I planned on where I could wear it.

The following weekend, we rose early to head down Washington State's I-5 to Oregon. During the hour trip, I ruminated on which color to choose and was a bit nonplused when Bob bypassed the mall and aimed the car toward the City Center. We'd never shopped in downtown Portland, but we were at a turning point in our marriage, so I was up for anything. Or so I thought.

"Why are we stopping at a pawn shop?" I asked.

"You'll see." Bob wore a proud smile.

"I'll stay in the car, if you don't mind," I said, thinking about my new dress.

He bounded off, a man on a mission. After that pawn shop, on to another. And another. An hour or so later, he stated, "Just can't find what I want."

By now I was a little more than curious. "What are you looking for?"

"Supposed to be a surprise. Guess I'll have to order it." Although temporarily defeated, my husband was not beaten.

So while parked at the curb watching men staggering about, brown paper sacks clenched in their grimy hands, I pressed my husband for particulars about this surprise. I'd rather be surprised now than later when the object of his affection lay before me.

"A Winchester 243," he said.

"A what?"

"You gotta have something to hunt with," he explained.

So it was that I acquired a hunting rifle . . . and a new lifestyle. Truly, it drew me closer to my husband. An intimacy we'd never known before developed between us. There's something about being outdoors in driving rain, howling winds, and freezing snow that brings a man and a woman together. And I learned a lot about Bob. He was a great teacher of nature and how to read animal signs.

He also had a natural gift for directions. On one occasion we trudged what seemed like miles deep into a forest. Towering firs dwarfed us.

"I need to rest," I huffed, out of breath and leg-weary. After unstrapping my fanny pack and propping my gun next to the trunk, I leaned against a tree and slid to the damp, moss-covered ground. Something else I learned about my husband is how patient he could be. He never rushed me or pushed me beyond what I could endure. He waited, never complaining, until I was ready to resume the hunt.

That night, after the two-hour drive home, I realized I didn't have my fanny pack, which contained my hunting license.

"We'll get it tomorrow," Bob said matter-of-factly.

"We'll never find it."

"I know right where we took a break."

"But that was in the middle of acres and acres of trees." I recalled the zigzagging we'd done, crossing creeks and climbing slopes—none of it in a straight line or even along a slightly imaginable path.

The next day Bob hiked directly to *that* tree! In spite of my excitement, he remained nonchalant. He rarely gets excited.

Yet on one particular day, I learned he could leap to drama. Again, way out in the woods, he parked his four-wheel-drive Ford.

Handing me a whistle to wear around my neck, he said, "Blow this if you get lost. Or if you need me. You shouldn't have to 'cause you can't get lost in here. This patch of firs is surrounded by logging roads on all four sides. It's not much more than an acre. Just walk straight through. I'll drive around and wait on the other side for elk you push out."

What Bob learned about me was that I *could* get lost in a postage-stamp-size patch of trees. After slipping down muddy creek banks, catching shoe strings on woody spikes and catapulting through the air, crossing that creek bank again and again, and blowing that stupid whistle practically nonstop, I finally emerged at the exact spot where he'd dropped me off. Walking down the logging road to join him was a no-brainer.

He was quite animated when he spied me coming. He launched into a lively monologue about how long I'd been in there, and why didn't I blow the stupid whistle, and how in the world could I get lost in a dinky patch of foliage, and how he was never going to let me go off by myself ever again.

Thank heavens for that!

So the togetherness of hunting continued. Now it was time to plunge into the next item on the list of What-I-Can-Join-My-Husband-In. Since we'd never had a honeymoon, for our twenty-fifth anniversary we went halibut fishing in Alaska.

Today, skidding around the corner is our thirty-eighth anniversary, and for a second honeymoon Bob consented to a Caribbean cruise. Hallelujah! For years I've tried to sell him on the finer points of a cruise. A few months ago, out of nowhere, he announced, "I'll go on a cruise with you." That proves you *can* teach an old dog new tricks.

We're both old dogs now. And the marriage keeps getting better. Thankfulness doesn't begin to touch my sentiment about Bob's twentieth anniversary "swan song" that turned out to be the opposite of a "swan song" in the fabled sense of the word.

I no longer have that beautiful jade necklace with the swans swimming together. A few months ago a burglar broke into our house and stole it. But the thief didn't make off with the necklace's message, which will remain forever wrapped around my heart.

−MARY ELLEN STONE

Why do we get married in the first place? A big part of it is the longing to be with the person we've fallen in love with. We want to spend our days and nights together as much as possible.

It's so easy to lose sight of that! Everyone else in the world clamors for our time and attention. He does "his thing," she does "her thing," and soon a couple who once couldn't stand to be apart from each other during a normal workday are traveling in completely separate universes.

Then we wonder why we don't seem to be connecting anymore.

Whether we've been married two months or twenty years, we periodically need to check our priorities list and our activities list. And sometimes we just need to say no to the others so we have time to say yes to the one we love.

After all, we can't experience togetherness if we're not spending time together!

$\mathcal{A}$ Desire That Burned Slowly

It was getting late, and my husband would be heading to bed soon. As long as I kept our baby up just a little longer, I could avoid that which I dreaded most—the bedroom.

Funny, you hear so many women talk about how much they love sex and how they have "needs." But for me, a newlywed with a baby attached to my hip most of the time and laundry piled in our closet—not to mention the huge rings that had grown around both of our bathtubs and needed cleaning—sex was about as appealing as a root canal.

It wasn't just that I was tired. Sure, I liked to pretend that was it, but it was more than that. Having dipped my toes into the world, so to speak, in my early years by dabbling in promiscuity and a series of pointless relationships, I found that sex had become painful, shameful, and dirty. And every time my husband reached out to touch me, countless faces filled my mind and reminded me of just how dirty I had become.

Unfortunately, my husband didn't understand my complete disgust with sex and assumed something was wrong with him. I could see the pain in his eyes every time I turned him down, and even though it broke my heart to hurt him, I just couldn't make that step to accept his sexual advances.

Fortunately God saw my pain and our need for intimacy, and began to chisel away at the walls that I had carefully placed around my heart.

My healing began at a marriage conference.

The entire conference seemed to be about sex. Obviously, this made me very uncomfortable because I was hearing, from a strong Christian couple, that sex was not only good and healthy, but was actually designed by God to create intimacy in marriage.

They also spent a great deal of time talking about things that polluted the marriage bed, including previous relationships. This portion of the seminar got my attention and helped me see the root cause of my unwillingness to have sex.

The speaker attached two pieces of paper with some glue and let them dry for a moment while he read 1 Corinthians 6:18, " 'Run from sexual sin! No other sin so clearly affects the body as this one does. For sexual immorality is a sin against your own body.' " He explained that sex joins two people just like glue joins paper. Then he ripped the pages apart. The result—two shredded pieces of paper. This was an "Aha!" moment because it showed me why I felt so ripped apart in this area. I realized that my previous relationships were affecting my intimacy with my husband.

I have often heard it said that healing starts with pain. For me, this was definitely true. Once I admitted and confessed my sin, God began to pour His truth into my heart, telling me that I was a new creation in Him and that there was no condemnation in Christ Jesus.

He also continued to place me in situations where I heard godly men and women speak openly about the marriage bed, which not only removed a great deal of the shame I had previously associated with sex, but also opened my heart to the possibilities for intimacy that God had for my marriage.

It wasn't like God suddenly snapped His fingers, turning everything hot and heavy in an instant. It took time—a long time—to become comfortable with myself, my husband, and our sexuality. And this is where prayer came in.

By then I knew I was free from my past sins and I understood just how important sex was to our marriage, but somehow my heart just wasn't in it. So I started to pray, sometimes even while my husband and I were making love.

I prayed that God would give me a burning desire for my husband and I prayed that He would help me love my husband in this way. And God answered that prayer. Not that everything is perfect now; I still have a tendency to hide behind past hurts and shame. But now I know how to get beyond those feelings.

When I feel vulnerable, I turn to God and ask for His help. I have also learned to share my feelings, openly and honestly, with my husband. He, in turn, makes a point to be very gentle and patient with me. Sometimes that means taking things slow and other times that means giving me advance notice of his desires so I can come into the bedroom mentally prepared, but it has all been worth it because the end result has been a mutually fulfilling and very intimate sex life.

–J. F. BUNGER

God created humans to be sexual beings. He created us for intimacy with another human and oneness within the safeguards of marriage. While sex may not be the traffic-stopping, end-all experience the movies portray, sex is a good gift, created not just for procreation but also for us to enjoy.

There are times in our lives, however, when sex just isn't

pleasurable. Sometimes, as J. F. found, it's because of previous sexual encounters, or it may be because of childhood sexual abuse. Sometimes sex stops being a blessing because of physical problems or even medication.

God designed sex to be a good thing that helps hold our marriages together when times get tough. When it stops being a good part of life, there's no shame or embarrassment in getting help. Doctors, pastors, and counselors alike realize the importance of sex. All are used to helping couples work through emotional or physical difficulties.

As we have patience with each other's needs and desires, and seek help, we can enjoy each other's bodies as an extension of our communication, as God designed.

Slow to Anger

On my way out I slammed the door so hard it rocked the small, cramped trailer.

"I'm going to the hardware store and I'll be back when you see me!"

As I marched away, I realized the noise woke up our newborn son, who began to wail.

Serves her right, I thought. *Now she can take care of him.*

Norma and I had been married three years. Our first year had gone fairly well in civilian life. The freshness of being newly married and juggling my night job with her day job kept us busy.

Then I joined the Army and was sent to Germany. There was much to see and learn in a foreign country, and being able to bring my wife along seemed like an extended vacation. However, as time progressed, we focused on planning new activities and adjusting to new roles instead of building a relationship with each other.

When my tour of duty in Germany ended, the Army reassigned me to Fort Benning. To our delight, our son was born shortly after our arrival there. This put a screeching halt to any semblance of normalcy and forced us to focus on never-ending baby activities.

More frequent trips to the Laundromat, late-night feedings, and walks to quiet our son's ever-increasing colic depleted us of energy. Doctors told us that our son might have undue pressure on the brain because of his enlarged head, so we endured stress while our baby was continually poked and prodded by various doctors. Then a strangulated inguinal hernia resulted in surgery at four months of age. Thankfully, this alleviated much of his discomfort, and we learned his enlarged head was normal for our family. It seemed our baby had taken first place in my wife's heart, though, and the divide between us kept growing. The demands of the military did not help, either. *Once we get back home where my old job is waiting for me and we are closer to our families, things will get better,* I told myself.

Being released from the military did bring relief, but I carried my old expectations and attitudes back to my hometown with us. I went back to full-time civilian employment, but things at home were still rocky.

The airline job I returned to paid better than the military, but I still felt unfulfilled. So, having a love for young people, I decided to volunteer with a youth hot-line program one evening a week. Even though we had one car at the time, I told Norma, "You can just drive me there if you need to use the car."

Of course that meant she had to wake up and bring our toddler to pick me up late at night.

Every week at the crisis center, I met with a team of six other people and we answered phone calls from teens who needed help, whether they were having trouble with homework, were distraught over acne, or were depressed and talking about thoughts of suicide.

When Norma came to pick me up, often I was oblivious to her problems because my own trauma consumed me.

We both had strong personalities, and on more than one occasion my German temper and her Irish temper had led to volatile situations. Both of our fathers had similar tempers and had unknowingly mentored and molded us, so we lacked positive coping skills. When things did not go my way, I would just explode.

I blamed Norma's moodiness on the tension between us, only to find out that she was pregnant with our precious second child. I felt she had unrealistic expectations of me—such as reading her mind—which caused friction. For example, she would say things like, "You need to take out the trash." How was I supposed to know that she meant that very instant? I figured later that day or the next would be soon enough. I did not know that her daily frustrations had built to the point that she was seriously contemplating a divorce.

While driving a cargo truck on the tarmac at work one day, I was listening to my radio. The station that I could hear best at the airport was a religious one. I was not a religious man but was riveted by a preacher who talked like anyone could know God personally.

I started tuning in daily; the preacher would bring up things that made me think he must be looking in our windows at home. He said things like, "Selfishness can fuel relational fires, and when we act in harshness it only fans the flames," and "The Bible explains that giving quiet words instead of harsh ones can put out those fires."

After a week or so of listening to these powerful facts, I suggested to Norma, "Let's go hear this preacher in person."

I started attending the church weekly and quickly learned that this preacher made Bible truths come alive.

We noticed that as we continued to attend the church, our home atmosphere began to change. We started applying the principles we heard by turning them into actions, and we started feeling more loving toward each other. The pastor would say things like, "If you stick your finger with a pin, that action causes pain." Then he would apply spiritual truth. "When we stab people with harsh words, that action causes pain, and when people are in pain, they will respond by lashing out."

We began using God's truths in raising our two children. Norma and I committed to follow Jesus' ways, and our love for Him began healing our own love for each other.

As we grew closer to God and each other, my quick temper began to bother me. I no longer wanted to hurt Norma with harsh words and actions. I began an all-out attack against my anger. I scoured the Bible for God's words about anger, wrath, and self-control. I discovered that if I did not guard my mouth, I would see chaos and destruction in my home.

My anger had a strong grip over me, but God's love and truth were stronger. By His grace, my volatile temper eventually became a thing of the past.

With my anger in check, I was able to focus on Norma and her needs. Words like, "Honey, can I get you something while I'm up?" and actions like listening to her while she poured her heart out at midnight—even though I had to get up early the next day—let Norma know she was my priority.

Almost forty-five years have passed since we first began our marriage journey together. We have a passion for each other that makes our early years pale in comparison. It seems a lifetime ago that those doors slammed in anger, but the doors of our hearts have opened and remain open because of God's love.

–DON SULTZ

One of the most destructive forces in a marriage is anger and the accompanying harsh words. When we fail to control our tempers, what we often really say to a spouse is, "I'm more important than you are, and I don't care if I hurt you."

"Well, my mate makes me angry," some people counter.

But that's not true. Sure, others can goad us, but we still choose how we'll react.

Living with someone who expresses a lack of self-control can be exhausting and can squelch the flames of love. And when we're the person with anger issues, that, too, can seem overwhelming. Such habits are hard to break!

It may be difficult to control anger and harsh words—but it's not impossible. As Don found, one key element is turning to Scripture for guidance and memorizing the words that will help us maintain control. And when a short temper is an issue in our lives, most of all, we have to turn to God to help us maintain control and express love.

It's Okay to Rock the Boat

I sat alone that evening. My tea had gone cold. Kevin, my son, was asleep. The clock sounded like a metronome. Dazed, I replayed the message from Steve's boss. He had called to say he was sorry Steve was sick. I knew Steve wasn't sick, but where was my husband? Sometimes he stayed overnight since he drove several hours to work. Just yesterday he told me he'd stay overnight, avoiding the long commute two days in a row.

"Sick?! Yeah, right!" We had just spent a wonderful Christmas with our son Brian and his family, and they had returned home two days ago. Hours stretched long into the night. I was baffled. Finally I heard Steve's car in the driveway.

After our customary hug and kiss at the door, I numbly blurted out, "Your boss left a message on the voice mail."

Tension pulled Steve's face taut. "A message?"

"Yes. He was sorry you were sick and unable to come to work." I stared at him. I couldn't help but have a flashback of the man I fell in love with in college, the thrill of saying wedding vows before friends and family, bearing and raising our three sons. Like sand, it all slipped between my fingers in that instant.

"Well, Jan, I guess you know I wasn't at work these last two days."

Through the night we talked. In brutal honesty, he told me about the secret side of his life. My stomach wrenched as he told me he'd been with the woman he now loved as a result of an office romance. He suggested I could file for a divorce.

Daylight couldn't come soon enough. I needed to call our pastor and pour my heart out to him. My world had collapsed and I wanted to die! In six months we would have been married for forty-three years. We were faithful members of our very large church, and Steve was on the church board of directors.

When I told our pastor what had happened, he was shocked. In an effort to confront Steve, he sent two elders to our house. The doorbell rang and my husband was indeed surprised! With a diabolical expression of anger I'd never seen, he ran out the back door and sped away in his car. This was December 31, and New Year's Eve had turned into a nightmare!

News of our crisis spread quickly through the church, and the board held sessions of prayer and fasting for my husband. Our church family reached out to support my son and me through prayer. Kevin, our thirty-two-year-old son with Down's syndrome, lives with me and needs special care. I explained to him that Daddy didn't love me, but that he loved him very much and that wouldn't change. Every week he would ask the pastors and his Sunday school class to pray for his dad to come home.

Steve moved out of our house and into an apartment less than two miles from us. For almost three years he came to our home for part of each weekend. He provided for our material needs, and he called almost every morning to see if we were doing okay. Each encounter was a painful reminder of his absence. The heaviness of depression would hit me at any time. I wouldn't want to do anything but just sit for hours.

We had married right after college, and I depended on my husband for everything. Neither of us realized we needed effective relationship tools for a healthy marriage. Didn't everyone just settle into life after the honeymoon and live happily ever after? We weren't aware how limited our communication skills were. I was busy with three small boys; Kevin, the youngest child, needing constant special attention. I put my energy into raising the children and left almost everything else to my husband. He held a stressful job in the computer field and learned, through many failed attempts, that I was unwilling to understand his business world and unable to empathize with his workplace challenges.

A young woman at his job, however, provided a listening, compassionate ear. The rest, as they say, is history. Over the next ten years their relationship grew, and he became increasingly emotionally distant from our family.

"Don't rock the boat" was a response I had learned early as a child. My reaction to problems was to look the other way and hope they might just go away. My greatest fear in life was that my husband would leave and I would have to make my own way. Someone had always taken care of me.

Over the years I'd seen several hints that he was seeing someone else, but I was afraid to confront him. Terrified to hear the truth, I only buried myself in raising the boys, leaving no room for my husband. We were still a family unit and I could only think of one thing: "Don't rock the boat."

By not confronting Steve, my greatest fear materialized—I was left alone. He suggested again, one year later, that I could pursue a divorce. However, I took my wedding vows seriously; I made a promise before God and others that I would love and cherish Steve, for better or for worse. Our two older sons had families of their own and lived in distant states. Our special-needs son faced various physical and emotional health challenges that I dealt with alone.

Handling financial issues on my own required some help and advice from church members knowledgeable in those areas.

I rarely pick up the Bible and start reading where the page falls open, but shortly after Steve left, one day I did just that. The Bible opened to Philemon, a book I had never read, and verse 15 caught my eye. Paul mentioned to Philemon that his slave Onesimus was separated from him for a little while so that Philemon might have him back for good.

I hung on to that. "Lord, could this be you telling me what you have planned?" Dare I think it could be prophetic for me? I believed it was!

On the advice of our pastors, I began seeing a Christian counselor. She gently guided me to see ways I could become a stronger, more self-confident person. I knew who Mrs. Stephen Lucas was, but not who Jan Lucas was. One day my counselor asked me to list my strengths and weaknesses. I listed numerous weaknesses, but few strengths. Slowly and skillfully as she counseled me, my long list of perceived weaknesses eventually became strengths. I began to feel good about the person I was becoming.

The first summer I was alone, I decided to build a small lap harp. I love music and am good with my hands, so that seemed like a fun way to pass the time. I intended for the harp to be just a conversation piece in my home, but then I received the opportunity to become a Hospital Certified Harp Therapist. I took lessons, studied hard, and graduated as a therapist two years later. I started to play my harp at the hospital to comfort others.

I soon realized that reaching out to others was very healing for me. The heavy cloak of depression lifted when I ministered to others. That year I also took tap dancing lessons. I joined a weight-loss program and returned to my wedding-day weight.

With the guidance of my counselor, I learned how to communicate and confront in healthy, effective ways, and my self-confidence increased. Steve saw these very dramatic differences, and he became attracted to the efficient, confident person I had become.

During the third year we were apart, Steve started reading devotionals and books on relationships and studying Scripture. One night, nearly three years after he left our family, he asked me if I would consider taking him back. He told me he had been watching me grow and mature (yes, even at age sixty-five), and he was very attracted to the new person I had become.

The books and Scripture he read showed him that he was living a life that greatly displeased God, and he was willing to do whatever it took to gain my trust and reconcile our relationship.

During our separation, God had been changing both of us dramatically. Steve changed from being self-centered to being unselfish. He learned to be in touch with his emotions and express his feelings. In forty-four years of marriage I had never seen him cry, and now I began to wonder if he would ever stop! He became humble and repentant and apologized to everyone we knew for what he had done. Steve met face-to-face with family members and asked for forgiveness. I began to love this new man more than I ever dreamed possible!

During our period of reconciliation, we attended weekly sessions with a marriage counselor and went to a marriage seminar where we gained valuable tools we needed to have a healthy relationship, especially in the area of communication. We both read books on relationships like they were water to parched souls.

On New Year's Eve, three years to the day after our nightmare encounter, my husband moved back to our home. He had regained my trust, and the reconciliation process was complete. He proved he was willing to do whatever it took to make things right. We renewed our wedding vows on Valentine's Day.

—JAN LUCAS, AS TOLD TO CHERYL FREEMAN

What do you do when it looks like a love may not last forever after all? Well, as Jan learned, there are a few things you don't do . . . like don't assume God is no longer at work.

And don't play "Taps" on the marriage too soon.

Humans are fickle. And even when Satan is trying to destroy a marriage, the Holy Spirit is still able to get into the little crevices of even the hardest heart.

Meanwhile, when the glue of a marriage comes unstuck, it's an opportunity for us to turn to God afresh for guidance. No matter what a spouse does, we can make sure that our lives are right where God wants us to be. When a spouse marches out the door, God enters our lives in a whole new way. God delights in bringing hope into hopeless situations and working miracles.

So anytime anything negative happens in your marriage, don't stop praying, don't stop believing, and don't give up. Because you never know what God has in store.

Sleepless in
Seattle

I lay in bed staring at the darkness. My husband, Larry, snored softly beside me. We'd just had another fight. I could hardly remember what started it, but we'd both said ugly, hateful things. Nothing had been resolved. We'd just gotten tired. Now he slept and I lay here, feeling utterly alone.

I crawled out of bed to check on our two sons. David, such a handful while awake, looked like an angel even though his face was sticky from the ice cream he'd eaten earlier. I pulled Matthew's covers back on his small body and smoothed his blond head. He needed a haircut. Working full time with two small sons to referee and a house to keep clean, I never had enough time to do it all.

Something drew me to the window. I could see the lights from downtown Seattle. So many people. What were they doing? Were they as lonely as I was? Was there anyone out there who cared?

God, I cried, *help me find the strength to leave.*

After ten years of marriage, I wanted out. Our love hadn't died in the heat of this battle or any other battle. It had died at the bottom of a wall it couldn't climb.

I remember clearly the day I laid the first brick. We'd been married nine months. We went to a movie and I waited for Larry to reach over and take my hand, thus proving the magic was still there. But he didn't and, as the movie progressed, I grew hurt and angry. He shrugged it off, surprised I was upset over such a little thing. To him it was nothing; to me it was the first sign our love wasn't perfect.

As the years passed, I added more bricks. When we were first married, he called me every day from work. But slowly those phone calls grew farther apart and finally stopped. When I brought it up, he started calling again, but it wasn't the same. When we watched TV in the evening, he'd fall asleep. When we went out for dinner, he couldn't think of anything to say. His days off were measured by how much he got done—chores, work, and the children took priority. I got the crumbs, and I was starving.

I felt guilty for feeling the way I did; he wasn't abusive, he didn't run around with other women, he didn't drink or do drugs. He came home every night and worked hard to support our family. Despite this, the wall grew, built with bricks of buried anger, unmet needs, silences, and cold shoulders. The marriage books we read made things worse; counseling confused the issues.

Divorce seemed like the only answer. It would give me a chance to start over and find the *right* person. Yes, it would be hard on the children, but when I was finally happy, I'd be a better parent. In the long run, it would be better for all of us.

Before taking that big step, I asked myself some key questions. First, would a divorce make me happier? Somewhere I read that people who divorce tend to remarry the same kind of person; that the root of unhappiness isn't in the people we marry but in ourselves.

When I looked at my husband, I knew this was true. The trait in Larry that drew me to him—his calm exterior—also drove me crazy.

He never complained, criticized, or caused a fuss. The downside was that when situations arose when he *should* get angry, he didn't.

Once he was cheated in a business deal. I wanted him to confront the man who'd lied to him, but he wouldn't. His love of peace kept him from standing up for himself, making me think he was a moral marshmallow. But if I divorced Larry, I knew I'd probably marry someone with his same peaceful demeanor. And if I did, my problems would be multiplied by his kids, my kids, child support, and custody battles.

I took a long, hard look at the single mothers I knew. They were exhausted and lonely. There was no one to help soothe crying babies, entertain toddlers, shuttle kids to practices, or help with the house, yard, and car.

Could I afford a divorce financially? According to my paralegal friend, a divorce could cost about twelve thousand dollars. My salary was good, but when I looked at our household expenses, there would be hardly enough money to live on, let alone extra money to pay lawyers.

Would my children really be better off in the long run? I looked at the children of my friends who'd divorced. Many of these kids started getting into trouble: staying out all night, drinking, doing drugs, and running away. Most of them were angry and blamed themselves for their parents' split. They took it out on their mother. The father became the hero because he wasn't doing the disciplining. Instead, he brought presents, bought a hot car, and took them fun places the mother couldn't afford. I'd heard that even twenty-five years after a split, children can still have significant emotional problems stemming from their parents' divorce.

What about my friends? I assumed they'd be there for me, but was I being realistic? Four of my friends divorced in one year—I didn't see any of them now. Two of them disappeared, one began leading a lifestyle I couldn't support, and another dated men I didn't care for. Even with the best of intentions, if I divorced, I'd probably lose many, if not all, of my friends.

God showed me I might escape my current pain, but in the long run, divorce extracted a high price. One I wasn't willing to pay.

But I refused to settle for the status quo. From experience, I knew I couldn't change my husband. There was only one person I could change: me. Jesus said, "You hypocrite, first take the plank out of your own eye, and then you will see clearly to remove the speck from your brother's eye" (Matthew 7:5 NIV). I got involved in a women's Bible study and started applying what I learned. Before I read a passage, I asked God to examine me. After many sessions on my face before Him, honestly asking for forgiveness, I started to change. I became less critical and more forgiving. I stopped taking everything Larry said and did so personally.

I tried new things—taking a writing class, asking a new friend to lunch, volunteering at school. With Larry's blessing, I quit my job to stay home with our children, even though it meant cutting our income in half.

From 1 Corinthians 13, I discovered love isn't a feeling but an action. I decided to treat Larry with love even though I didn't feel like it. Instead of pointing out his shortcomings, I told him the things he did right. Instead of reading books to see what Larry should be doing differently, I read to discover how I could be a better wife, mother, and friend.

My change in attitude had an amazing effect on Larry. He began spending more time with me. When I stopped overreacting to his comments, he felt freer to share more with me.

My decision to stay went against everything the world told me. Jesus promised, "I have come that [you] may have life, and have it to the full" (John 10:10 NIV). I decided if God was my God, then I could trust this promise. I asked Him to restore my love.

The love I thought had died didn't return in a week, a month, or even a year. There were times I wanted to give up. But I clung to God's promise that He would give me the desire of my heart.

One weekend Larry and I went away. Before we left, we prayed and drew a line in the sand. Everything that had happened before was over; this was a new beginning. That weekend I experienced a new passion for my husband. The flame I thought was dead was rekindled.

Today when I sit in church worshiping God, I shudder at what I almost threw away. Larry and I laugh over the things that used to drive me nuts, like his falling asleep in front of the TV. I can tell Larry anything, and he listens. Just yesterday he sent me a fax just to tell me he loves me.

At night when we lie curled up together, I reach over and touch him just to reassure myself he's still there. The love I have is strong. It's born out of suffering and obedience. The pain, tears, and struggles to get to this point were worth it for these rich rewards. There *is* hope for loveless marriages. Our relationship is living proof.

–JUDY BODMER

*A*re you a bricklayer? Most of us are, at some point or another. Like Judy, we let ourselves react to pain by keeping a little reminder of it, like a brick, in our brains and our hearts. Before long, the wall seems too high to climb over and can even obstruct our view of who our beloved really is.

It takes time and a lot of bricks to build a big wall. Likewise, it takes time, a lot of energy, and determination to deconstruct the wall. Complimentary words, kind acts, sweet attitudes—these are some of the tools that can help us deconstruct those walls. Then we have to be determined, with God's grace, not to put the bricks back when they come down.

And perhaps each day we should consciously evaluate: Am I building a wall today? Or a bridge?

A Glimpse of Shining Armor

Late again. I flipped my cell phone closed and shoved it back into my purse.

Third time this week, too.

"Was that Dad?" My ten-year-old daughter, Kiri, gathered her school things as we pulled into the driveway.

"Yep. He has to work late tonight."

My husband, Bruce, had always been somewhat of a workaholic, sometimes putting in eighty-hour weeks when his company's product absolutely had to be shipped by a certain date. But when he took this new job in Northern California, I'd hoped we could have a more normal life.

I drove the car into the garage and Kiri helped me bring the groceries inside. Together, we made the lasagna, salad, and garlic bread. But with just the three kids and me again, the dinner seemed tasteless.

Later that night when Bruce finally arrived home, I set a plate of leftovers on the dining room table and plopped into a chair across from him. He looked tired and I should have waited for a more appropriate time, but I blurted out angrily, "Is this the way it's going to be? I thought you said we'd have more time together when you took this job. You always choose work over us."

Bruce's shoulders slumped and he took a deep breath. "I told you it'd be a busy week."

"Yeah, you told me." I plunked my elbows onto the table and glared at him. "But it seems like it's always a busy week."

"That's not fair. Last week I got home at six each day." Bruce put his fork down and frowned, as if trying to remember. "Oh, and the week before we had a four-day work week."

I stood and stomped toward the kitchen. "That's 'cause it was Labor Day," I called from the other room.

That argument played out intermittently for the next three years. We'd reached an impasse. Bruce insisted that all of his hard work was for the family, to make a better life for us, pay down our credit cards, build our 401(k). I countered with the usual feminine argument: If you loved us, you'd spend more time with us.

It rankled in me. Surely Bruce could just tell his boss that today he was going to go home at a decent hour. Either he didn't have the backbone to stand up to the guy, or worse, Bruce would rather spend his time hanging out with his business associates.

That niggling doubt about Bruce's love continued to plague me. Even though he and I took the kids on wonderful family vacations, shared enjoyable times at the dinner table, served at church together, worshiped together, entertained together, and snuggled together, still, I harbored resentment about his long hours at work.

That doubt showed up in my attitude toward him. Sometimes it was hard to be pleasant, even though my husband is one of the sweetest men I know. Once the thought that work was more important to him settled into my brain, it was nearly impossible to remove. I started to look for proof that I was the low man on Bruce's totem pole. And each time he cautiously announced that he would have to travel or work late, I responded with exasperation.

One early spring afternoon Bruce called from his cell phone to tell me he'd be home in just a few minutes. I was tempted to reply sarcastically about his actually arriving home early, but something in his tone warned me to hold my tongue.

Ten minutes later we sat on the living room couch and held each other.

I felt sick inside. "So the rumors were true? They're actually going to lay off everyone?"

"Mm-hmm." Bruce squeezed my shoulder harder. "First the executives, then the managers, and then on down from there."

I'd seen this kind of thing on TV, but I couldn't believe it was happening to us in Smallville, USA. A hostile takeover of Bruce's company.

"How much time do we have?"

"Four weeks." Bruce took a deep breath. "We'll be okay. I've got a good severance package and the lady in HR says my rèsumè looks great. Guess I should call my headhunter." He stood up and headed for the phone.

Weeks went by with no new job prospects. Bruce did everything the job-seeking experts advised him to do, and still no interviews. Jobs for a highly qualified and experienced manager in the field of optics were slim in Northern California.

We put our beautiful house on the market and had a firm offer within a week. We stayed in our home till June, just long enough for Kiri to complete seventh grade and our middle son, Garrett, to graduate from high school. With no job prospects, we moved back to our previous hometown in Colorado and rented a small house.

Months passed. Bruce's severance package ran out. We'd agreed we wouldn't touch the money in savings that we'd made from the sale of our house. But after a year, we needed to use those funds, too.

Bruce set up a home office and began work as a mortgage broker. I taught music lessons and worked part time at our church in children's ministry. Since we were both self-employed, we needed to buy our own health insurance. When we found out that chronic health conditions would make insurance cost nearly two thousand dollars a month, I felt like crying. Without health insurance we would never be able to afford medications for my daughter and me, let alone the necessary visits to doctors and specialists.

My husband went out that very day and got a full-time job at a local lube shop. It would take ninety days to get health insurance, but we would be covered after that.

We'd sold one of our cars, but a friend from church gave Bruce a serviceable bicycle, and he rode that each day to work and back. If it hurt his pride, this former manager of hundreds of employees, to stand outside the lube shop and wash windows and vacuum out cars, Bruce never complained. Kiri and I needed health insurance and this was a way to get it.

At the end of each month Bruce took home a whopping $120. After taxes, the rest of his salary went to pay our health insurance premium.

Bruce worked at the lube shop for over a year, riding his bike through the cold Colorado winter. When he returned home each evening, I fed him dinner and then he climbed the stairs to his office and spent several more hours doing mortgage work.

On his days off, he also did consultations for optical companies in the area.

After two years, Bruce's job search landed him an excellent position. He still works long hours and travels occasionally, but I rarely complain anymore. I've learned a new kind of respect for my man, and I tell him fairly often, "Thank you for working so hard for me."

I used to think a husband was a man who would bring me flowers, speak romantic words every day, hold me when I'm scared, play with the kids, fix broken things, and work a forty-hour week. I wanted a husband who would love me the way I envisioned love.

But I've discovered that God has put into the heart of my man a much greater definition of love than I could have imagined. Life can be brutal, uncertain, and frightening at times. A man who will lay his life down daily to provide for and protect his wife and children demonstrates a love that transcends mere romance. He is the kind of hero whose shining armor is hidden under jeans and a Kmart T-shirt.

—DENA NETHERTON

What's the proof that your mate loves you?

Often we long for sweet words or little gifts or a tender touch. Dena longed for Bruce to spend time with her. But Bruce's way of showing his love to Dena was to take care of her needs.

Each of us expresses love primarily in one of those five basic ways: words, gifts, touch, time together, or acts of service. This is called our "love language." It's the way we tend to give love, and the way we tend to feel loved.[1]

For each marriage to be successful, we need to learn to "speak" our spouse's love language. Just because a wife doesn't tell her husband that she loves him doesn't mean she doesn't care—she might be saying "I love you" with frequent hugs and kisses. Likewise, a husband might be saying "I love you" by keeping his wife supplied with her favorite soft drink, or bringing home other little tidbits she likes.

Learn how your husband or wife expresses his or her love, and remind yourself of that love language when you're in doubt. And learn to reciprocate in your spouse's language. You'll be amazed at how this improves your marital communication!

---

[1] Gary Chapman, *The Five Love Languages* (Chicago: Northfield Publishing, 1992).

The Wake-Up Call

Our oldest daughter, Elizabeth, had insisted on organizing the twenty-fifth anniversary party for us, despite our protests.

The fact that she had to convince us to celebrate the 2004 event spoke volumes about the state of our marriage. I'd actually dreaded the party, and for good reason. Abby, the youngest of our eight children, wasn't yet a year old and I hadn't relished the idea of playing hostess while caring for a demanding toddler. I also wasn't sure that ours was a marriage to publicly laud.

The day of the planned festivities began like so many others. Abby had climbed into our bed in the middle of the night, then tossed and turned restlessly, leaving us tired and cranky. The morning was marked by dissension, with David and I snapping at each other and the kids over the least little infractions.

The irony of our discord on that particular morning was not lost on me, yet I felt powerless to do anything about it. Irritation with each other had become the standard for our relationship.

Despite her fatigue, Abby resisted falling asleep on the way to the hall where the party was being held. As soon as we arrived there, she started fussing and pulling at my shirt, demanding to be nursed.

With the sigh that had become my mantra, I sat in the corner to discreetly feed her, while David greeted the guests alone.

Mid-party, frustrated by her disruptive behavior, I strapped Abby into a baby carrier on my back and left to walk around the building, hoping she'd fall asleep.

I was glad to get away from the smiling guests and well wishers. I resented their joviality. What did they know about my marriage, about my life? What did anyone know? Even David wasn't aware of how unhappy I'd become.

As I strolled in the hot sun, I felt more than the weight of Abby on me; I carried the heaviness of discontent.

Long after I felt Abby's head resting in slumber against my back, I continued walking, reflecting on the past twenty-five years. I'd gotten married at age nineteen and had my first child less than a year later. Those early years were the halcyon days of our marriage. We both attended college classes and worked part time, staggering our hours around each other's so our children never had to be in day care.

We lived a kind of surreal existence—playing house as college students and spending our off hours at a nearby restaurant, holding hands, drinking gallons of coffee, and talking while our toddler slid melting ice cubes across the tray of the high chair.

We continued our tag-team parenting until we'd both graduated and decided I'd stay home full time to care for the children. I took my last college finals from the hospital bed where I'd just given birth to our fourth child.

Nineteen years and four more children later, our marriage had deteriorated to the point that I no longer recognized the man across the dinner table from me. Gone were our days of holding hands and talking for hours. The conversations we did share were cursory at best. Our relationship was bogged down by juggling bills and babies.

I finally returned to the party, disheveled from the heat, Abby still asleep on my back. When it was time for a photo-op, she woke up and started crying again, jarring my already strained nerves. Even though Elizabeth took her to the other end of the room, I could still hear Abby's screams as we posed. Now, when I look at those pictures, I see the fakeness of my smile and the look in my eyes, like a deer caught in the headlights of a car just before being hit.

That party should have been a wake-up call, prompting me to do something about the dismal state of our marriage. But I was too busy, too stressed, and too emotionally drained to attempt the upheaval of change. If I thought about the state of our relationship at all, it was in the context that we could work on it later, when the kids were grown. Instead, my husband's cancer diagnosis in June 2006 triggered a transformation.

The doctor's words to David, "You have cancer," shocked both of us. In the car on the way home from that appointment, I realized that a future without David was a bleak prospect. Time seemed to lag between the day of his diagnosis and David's surgery two weeks later, or perhaps I just finally slowed my own frantic pace.

I started spending less time on mundane household tasks and more with David. On different occasions during those two weeks we lay quietly on our bed, my head on his chest, listening to his heartbeat.

I started to remember why I had fallen in love with him in the first place. Would it be too late to change our relationship?

I visited David daily for the eleven days he spent in the hospital after an invasive surgery that removed the tumor on the back of his tongue and thirty-two lymph nodes in his neck. David couldn't speak for eight days and could only communicate by writing on a dry-erase board. In our verbal sparring, I'd always hurried him to get to the point. Now I patiently waited while he struggled to write.

Ironically, without much verbal communication, we connected on a much deeper level. I had to search his beautiful brown eyes for every nuance of meaning, pleased when I could guess what he needed just by his gestures. Mostly I held his hand while he drifted in and out of sleep. As he dozed, I had plenty of time for contemplation. My children not only survived my absence while I visited David, they thrived under the watchful care of my family. I wondered why I had let myself lose sight of my husband while I'd immersed myself so deeply in intensive mothering.

I began preparing for hospital visits with extra attention— slathering on fragrant lotion after showering, applying makeup and arranging my hair, then raiding the back of my closet for dresses and skirts. Liberally spraying myself with perfume one morning, I smiled as I realized I was courting my own husband.

When he was home the courtship continued. I became David's caregiver while he recovered from surgery, then during his radiation and chemotherapy treatments. I did things for him I would never have imagined doing—cleaning bloody wounds, changing dressings, doling out liquid feedings, and other unseemly tasks. These activities should have diminished any desire I felt for him, but the opposite was happening. For the first time in years, I was giving David my full attention, treating him with a tenderness that left grateful tears in his eyes.

Something truly wonderful developed between us during those months. I saw David's quiet strength as he dealt with pain. And his concern for his family's welfare overrode worries about his own situation. It became an honor and a privilege to care for my spouse. I fell in love with him all over again, and he, in turn, fell head over heels in love with this caring wife.

Every Wednesday for seven weeks in a row, I took advantage of generous offers of baby-sitting and supported David during the chemotherapy treatments that included a drug that exacerbated side effects. I became his comrade in the fight against cancer.

The days passed swiftly, one season blending into the next, until late fall when David could finally return to work. When I kissed him good-bye on his first day back, I clung to his thin frame. Before his cancer, I'd been so busy running the house, homeschooling, and tending small children, I practically shoved him out the door every morning so we could begin our day without him. He'd been just as eager to get away from squabbling children and a nagging, unhappy wife.

Now parting from each other held a bittersweet sadness. Not only had our love grown, but we'd also learned to enjoy each other's company. The initial tenderness of caring for each other had rapidly developed into a passion we hadn't experienced since our honeymoon days.

I wish it hadn't taken something as devastating as cancer to prompt us to change our relationship. I am convinced we could have stumbled along in a joyless marriage for several more years, neither unhappy enough to leave, nor miserable enough to do something about it. I know now that our marriage did not have to be like that, that it could have been better, if only we'd made an effort to put each other first in our lives.

In the years since his cancer, David and I have done things together I'd never even imagined. We schedule regular dates now, even if they often include a doctor's appointment. We sicken our children with our public displays of affection. Before, I often wondered what we would have to talk about after our children were grown and gone. Now I am excited about our future together as best friends.

June of 2009 marked three years since David's cancer diagnosis, and thirty years since our wedding. This time no one had to convince us to celebrate the milestone.

—MARY POTTER KENYON

*U*nfortunately a dramatic happening—often life-threatening—is the catalyst that finally moves us out of our ruts to work on our relationships.

But it doesn't have to be that way.

Are you unhappy with your marriage? Sit down with a piece of paper and dream. Write down what you think the ideal marriage would look like.

Now, how can you get there? Do you need to do a bit of courting? Bite back a few nasty words? Start caring about how you look when only your spouse sees you? Give affection? Bring home a treat once in a while?

Start today, start now. Don't wait until you're threatened by those events that might end your time together.

Give and You Shall Receive

I hung up the phone and fumed.

Why does Melissa have to call and brag every time her "perfect" husband sends her roses?

Well, to be honest, she didn't actually call me up just to tell me that—it was to ask me a question about something else. Then she told me about the flowers.

This subject just happened to be a sore spot with me. My husband, Jerry, had never sent me flowers—not even on my birthday or our anniversary. Oh, he always remembered those important days by giving me a special gift and taking me to dinner. But I wanted roses! Long-stemmed beauties standing tall and graceful in a lovely vase, set in a prominent place for everyone to see. Roses I could point to with pleasure, then announce proudly, "These are from my husband."

I realized that florist-delivered roses were expensive, and on our limited budget it was impractical to long for such frivolous acts.

But roses were also available in local supermarkets, and our budget could certainly afford those.

The root of my problem was that I was a romantic at heart. I felt if a man loved a woman, he sent her flowers. And if he *really* loved her, he sent her roses.

You say my husband may not have known about that rule? Well, he should have. I'd certainly given him enough hints through the years!

Only the previous month I had exclaimed, "I am so excited for Alexis!"

The newspaper hiding Jerry's face slid slowly down, just enough for me to see his eyes widen as he asked, "Why? Did she win the lottery?"

"No!" I answered. "Jim sent her a gorgeous bouquet of red roses today."

"Why?" he asked suspiciously, rattling his paper.

"For no reason at all."

"Hmmmm. I wonder what he did."

"He sent roses," I snorted. "I just told you."

"No, he must have done something bad and is trying to make it up to her."

I glared at him. He shrugged and quipped, "Well, that's what happens in the movies. Some guy cheats on his wife, feels guilty, and then sends her flowers."

"Jim would never cheat on Alexis, and you know it," I retorted. "*Some* men just happen to love their wives enough to do thoughtful things—like sending *flowers*."

"Seems like an awful expensive way to show their love. Why don't they just tell their wives they love them?"

"I'm sure they do. They're just evidently blessed with sensitivity greater than a donkey! They understand women enough to know what pleases them—unlike *some* men!"

Warming to the subject, I decided to toss my biggest hint. "I know I would certainly be thrilled if—"

Before I could finish, Jerry's cell phone rang. After talking for twenty minutes with his friend Bill about their upcoming golf trip, Jerry returned to his sports page. I sulked, but he never noticed.

Recalling my miserable failures at dropping hints, I thought, _No, I'm not about to mention Melissa's roses to him!_

Several weeks later, during a discussion about thoughtful husbands over coffee with my new friend Darcy, I admitted I had a great husband, but he'd be perfect if he'd surprise me with flowers—just once! She smiled and said, "I always get flowers, even on days that aren't special."

Oh no—not another one of those women with a perfect husband!

"That's great!" I responded, suddenly turning green and sorry the subject had arisen.

After a long silence she asked, "Wouldn't you like to know my secret?"

"Absolutely! If it works for me we'll market it and make a fortune."

She smiled broadly and said, "I get them myself."

"You've got to be kidding! What fun is that? You really buy your own flowers?"

"Why not? Don't you like flowers?"

"I love flowers, especially roses. But I want Jerry to buy them, order them from a florist, or just pick some up at the supermarket and surprise me with them. I'd feel so special!" Shaking my head, I concluded, "I certainly wouldn't feel special having to buy my own. I don't understand how you enjoy doing that!"

"Well, I do. My Glenn is a good, hardworking man, a loyal husband, and loving father to our children. So he isn't romantic in the flower department—I don't care. Besides, I love flowers. I can't grow them living in this townhouse, but why should I be deprived of their enjoyment just because they're not from my husband? So— when I want flowers I buy them."

Giving me a sideways glance she added, "The key is being able to do that without ruining your enjoyment by resenting the fact that your husband didn't get them for you."

"Hmmm. I never thought of it that way. Guess I need to work on that idea," I mused aloud, while thinking, *Not on your life!*

The next day I recalled Darcy's comments. I had to admit that my husband was hardworking, too, and when it came to being a good father, he won hands down.

Later that afternoon, while preparing Jerry's favorite meal of roast beef, mashed potatoes, homemade rolls, and gravy loaded with mushrooms, I smiled as I recalled another quality that endeared him to me.

For some reason I had the bad habit of running around barefoot after my bath instead of putting on my slippers. By the time I finally crawled into bed, my feet were like ice. Out of consideration I tried to keep them from touching him. But even if he was asleep, he roused immediately and said, "Honey, put your feet on my back so they can get warm."

"No, they'll freeze you!" I'd object. But he always grabbed my feet and pulled them up onto his toasty warm back. I cringed with guilt when I felt him flinch. He never complained. Once my feet were warmed, I snuggled even closer to him as my heart flooded with fresh love and thought how most men would probably just snarl and say, "Keep those icy feet away from me!" or "Why don't you wear your slippers?"

But not my man!

And when we went out he always made a point of telling me how beautiful I looked and how proud he was that I was his—words any wife would love to hear.

Kitty Chappell, I chided, *you have a wonderful husband! Darcy is right. What is the big deal if he doesn't send you roses when he has all of these other wonderful qualities?*

At dinner I ladled extra gravy over his mashed potatoes and kissed him on the head.

But I wasn't yet cured of my rose cravings.

A week later while shopping, I stopped in the florist section of the supermarket and admired a fresh shipment of long-stemmed roses. I had a sudden relapse and ached with longing. *I wish Jerry would send me roses.* Nudged by a sudden strong impulse, I reached for a dozen of the lushest red ones, enhanced with greenery and baby's breath, and added them to my cart. At home, I arranged them in a beautiful vase and placed them in the center of the kitchen island.

As I put the finishing touches on dinner that evening, I heard the garage door open and wondered what I'd say when Jerry asked about the roses.

Maybe I'll smile coyly and say, "They must be from a secret admirer—I don't know who else would send me flowers." Then I'll smile sweetly to take the sting out of my intended rebuke.

Or maybe I'd just keep him guessing for a while—give him a chance to get jealous. He might even feel guilty that I had to resort to buying my own roses—and voilà! He'd finally get the hint.

As Jerry walked into the kitchen, I turned to watch his expression. His eyes widened as they focused on the brilliant bouquet. "Who sent the roses?"

Fully intending to say, "A secret admirer," I was surprised at my response of, "I did."

Why did I say that—and now what do I do? I asked myself.

He stood there, puzzled. "Why would you send roses?"

Beats me! I thought. I was shocked further when I responded with, "They're for you."

"For me?" he said, stunned. Gently running his fingers over their velvety petals, he stammered, "They're beautiful—thank you." A sudden twinge of guilt stabbed me in the heart.

Then I stood in amazement as I watched Jerry's face suddenly crumple and tears form in his clear blue eyes. One brave tear escaped down his cheek as he shook his head and whispered softly, "No one has ever given me a dozen roses before."

I was dumbfounded! *Men like to receive roses from women?!*

I thought that was something only women wanted from men! Too stunned to speak, I just stood there.

In one stride, Jerry grabbed me in his arms, his wet cheek brushing mine, and whispered, "I don't know what I did to deserve this, but thank you so much, honey. I love you!"

The joy I received from giving Jerry those roses (even though I hadn't intended to) far surpassed any pleasure I would have felt if I'd received them from him. I rejoiced during the following week to hear him tell his friends, in person and on the phone, "You should see the beautiful roses my wife gave me—a dozen of them!"

And thereafter, on every birthday, anniversary, and Valentine's Day, I received a dozen beautiful roses from my open admirer—my "perfect" husband.

I learned two truths from this God-orchestrated event. One, it is indeed more blessed to give than to receive. And two, be willing to give what you really want from someone else but never receive—be it praise, a kind word, the benefit of the doubt, or roses.

−KITTY CHAPPELL

One of the most loved and most quoted verses of Scripture is Luke 6:31, "Do to others as you would like them to do to you." We're taught this basic concept from childhood on. But how many times do we really think about employing it in our marriage? What would you like today? Someone to bring you a cup of coffee, to pamper you? Then perhaps you should do those chores for your spouse. Would you like someone to give you the gift of a listening heart, an encouraging hug, or a few words of praise?

As we give, we find out that we get blessings in return—maybe not in the same way they were given, but in most cases, we enjoy a renewed closeness and tenderness with the one we love.

Forgiveness– With No Strings Attached

I remember clearly the day my world crashed. Ten years of marriage, our fourth daughter on the way, and a nice house had given me a false sense of security and happiness.

It was actually Christmas night when the initial blow fell. All was quiet as my husband and I climbed into bed at the end of our tenth Christmas celebration together. We talked quietly about the events of the day and about our children with their gifts. We laughed softly at the fond memories we'd created that day.

We had a good marriage. We were good friends before we got married, and that helped as we encountered trials along the way. However, I had sensed for about six months that something was bothering him, and I struggled to figure out what it was without asking him.

As we lay in bed that Christmas night, my husband said something that did not fit with the flow of the conversation: "I've had this problem for a long time. I've struggled with pornography use and I've never been able to stay away from it," he said just louder than a whisper.

I sat up in bed and exclaimed, "Honey, I knew something was wrong, but I couldn't figure out what! Don't worry. We'll learn how to beat this."

I then lay back down and held his hand. He said very little, but thanked me.

I learned later that he had not planned to confess. He was just as surprised as I was that those words came out of his mouth that night!

Since my husband had not planned on confessing or giving up his involvement with pornography, he awoke the next day feeling and acting strange and scared. Panic rippled through me. This was not the determined, straitlaced man I thought I had been married to for ten years. After he left for work, my world fell apart.

I went to bed and told my children I was not feeling well. While they enjoyed their new Christmas gifts, I prayed and cried and read Scripture. Each day when my husband came home from work, I could get up, fix dinner, and function for a while. He took care of the children and cleaning up after dinner. He knew that I was struggling to accept the bombshell he'd dropped on me. And he knew I was waiting for him to choose repentance. We remained cordial, despite the problem. The friendship that we had before we married was still present and helped us not hurt each other too much as we tried to process what was happening.

During my prayer time, I knew God was urging me to forgive, but it was difficult to forgive something I didn't understand. I bought books on pornography addictions and recovery and was reading them.

After spending a lot of time in prayer and meditation, I told my husband that he needed to confess to a minister and have a plan for beating the addiction if we were to stay together. I also pledged to support any recovery efforts on his part, but I wanted him to devise the plan.

After nearly two weeks, he hadn't done anything that I had asked, and I began to think I might actually have to kick him out of the house. I felt a need to protect my three daughters, not knowing what pornography had done to his mind through twenty years of involvement.

One day as I was crying and praying, I sensed the Lord telling me to call a certain friend and church member for help. My friend prayed with me, named books that I should read, and told me she had a certain level of experience with this in her own marriage.

"Deena, you absolutely must forgive him if you are going to help him," she insisted.

Confusion reigned. I wanted to forgive, but I didn't think I could. I resisted the idea that I should forgive before he confessed and repented. He caused the trouble, he should have to fix it, I reasoned. Then I could show love and forgiveness because then I wouldn't be as much at risk for hurt and rejection.

Early the next morning I cried through my prayer to forgive my husband and asked for strength to talk to him again about the issue.

I called him at work and left a message saying, "I love you and I'm still willing to help, but I need to see you taking steps to get help."

After the call, it was as if God had picked me up and was holding me. I was determined to forgive this man so he could feel my support. I still did not understand the addiction, but I realized I didn't need to understand it to forgive him.

In all of my prayers, though, God had not assured me that my husband would leave it all behind. He assured me that He would take care of our daughters and me, that He would bless me if I obeyed Him, but He did not say that I would get what I wanted out of all this. That was difficult to accept. I wanted to control the outcome of this situation, but I had to admit that I could not.

My husband called me back a short time later and cried as he thanked me for my continued support and love. When he arrived home that night, I knew something inside him had changed for good.

I called my friend back to tell her that I felt the immediate danger was over. She said she and her husband had prayed for two hours for our situation the day I had first called her. I could not believe that someone would care so much. Without a doubt, those prayers helped me to be determined to forgive my husband and make one last plea for his repentance.

A few days later, he confessed to a minister and we were on the rocky road to recovery. Eventually we were in Christian counseling that focused on forgiving past offenses and healing longtime wounds, even from childhood. That proved to be the catalyst for complete release from the hold pornography had on him. I can't say I enjoyed his journey to freedom from that addiction, but I can say that I enjoy his life as a free man!

My husband is very thankful to be on the other side of this issue. For years he doubted that it was possible to overcome this, but God found a way to convince him of the power of love and forgiveness.

—DEENA ANDREWS

The issue in your marriage may not be pornography, but since marriages are comprised of two humans, chances are that all of us, at one time or another, face a serious issue dealing with a mate's behavior. At some point in our marriages, most of us have to forgive our spouse.

That's easier said than done! It's especially difficult to forgive when the behavior we hate so much doesn't change. We would rather offer forgiveness as a reward for a spouse changing than as a free gift.

As Deena found, sometimes when we forgive without strings attached, changes happen. Sometimes they don't. That's when we have to turn to God and ask for grace to forgive as He does—unconditionally.

To err truly is human, and to forgive not only is divine, but takes divine help! It also brings a renewed sense of Christ-likeness into a marriage.

*F*rom Soup to Superb

We've all heard that the way to a man's heart is through his stomach, but when I kicked my boyfriend out of the kitchen, I wasn't very interested in cooking for my husband.

I know, married women aren't supposed to *have* boyfriends. But what I know and what I did are two different things.

Oh, I was still keeping up with the Christian image of a godly family—taking chocolate no-bakes to youth group, inviting couples over for spaghetti and Bible study, taking my best homemade rolls to church dinners.

And all the time I was hiding the fact that someone was in the kitchen with me, and that we were thinking about making beautiful music together.

Music was partly what got us in trouble in the first place. We both wrote songs and sang. We'd written and directed church musicals together. We'd sung on the same praise team. It was no surprise that before long we were also sharing our new songs with each other. Alone.

That kind of creativity is powerful.

He told me before I moved to another state that he was attracted to me. I think we both knew part of it was just the music.

Still, when this man visited our family for three weeks, we made use of my kitchen. He danced with me across the linoleum to records we'd checked out at the library. He serenaded me while I tried to impress him with the cherry pie I burned out of distraction. He tapped out a rhythm on my hands while I folded the dish towels, and that's when he whispered for the first time that he loved me.

I was playing house as much as I had been playing the happy Christian family. I was Susie Homemaker, trying to impress this man with my domestic skills as if my husband didn't exist and I was out to win bachelor number two. And it was working.

I was ecstatic. I was terrified. I was guilty. I was *loved*.

And I didn't know what to do.

Because I was also hungry—ravenous—for affection.

But there was this little matter of my being married. With three children.

So a battle ensued. My emotions and thoughts clashed as I waited to see whether feelings or common sense would win. But I knew it would really come down to my will.

Would I be willing to sacrifice my marriage and my children's sense of security for my own needs to be met? Or would I remember my marriage vows and keep the covenant I'd made before God?

Would I gamble on the promises of a man who had no employment or sense of responsibility or history of stability, yet melted me with love songs? Or would I insist that he go home and leave my ordered world as it had been before he came?

He wanted me to come away with him. Just pack up my children and leave my husband, Tracy, without a backward glance.

I could hardly bear the fight. I was shocked at the intensity of anger I felt toward God. It seemed He had tricked me into marrying someone who could never meet my needs, then dangled forbidden fruit right in front of my nose and insisted I had to resist my craving.

Everything I believed about God's goodness, being faithful in marriage, giving my children a happier home than I grew up in—all of it was being shaken.

And I knew that if I didn't decide something soon, I would go too far to turn back.

The fear of God compelled me, so I asked this man to leave. Without me and my children.

My anger gave way to buckets of tears. I couldn't do anything but lie on the couch and bawl. Tracy must have known what my struggle was about, but he couldn't verbalize or even consider something so hideous. So he kept going to work as usual while waiting for me to resume my duties. As if having dinner ready for him at the end of the day was going to make everything okay.

Finally, after three days of sobbing, I wiped my nose and started going through the motions of home life. Neither of us mentioned how weird the last three weeks had been. We just kept going. I was more hateful than ever and harbored a grudge against Tracy. He seemed to be the only hindrance to my happiness, and I resented his very presence.

I was still filled with turmoil because the other man and I still communicated. This stirred my soul with longing and confusion.

In the midst of my anguish, I continued to read my Bible, but only out of habit. Before I opened God's Word every morning, I would cry out my frustration, screaming that I didn't know why I was even bothering to read it. I was convinced He wouldn't speak to my heart, and even if He did, that I couldn't believe or trust Him. I feared He enjoyed my agony and took pleasure in snatching away what seemed to be so good.

One night after washing dishes I noticed Tracy in his chair reading something. I quickly realized he was holding a letter I'd written to this man and accidentally left out.

Everything froze. I could no longer hear my children playing in the next room. The light reflected off of Tracy's glasses, so I couldn't see the pain in his blue eyes. The metallic taste of fear and guilt filled my mouth. As I raised my hand to my forehead, the smell of Joy dishwashing liquid mocked me. And my meal sat like a rock in my gut.

I don't know how long I stood like a statue, but eventually we both found our voices. Even though the idea crossed my mind to deny any wrongdoing since the letter wasn't explicit, I rejected it. I was weary of guarding every facial expression and conversation, weary of the fear of discovery as my constant companion.

So I finally told Tracy everything that had happened between the other man and me.

I thought Tracy's heart would break, but even that didn't soften me. I believed he deserved misery as much as I did because he'd withheld affection from me all our married lives.

And I was certain that my obedience to God was signing my own life sentence of misery.

Yet God surprised me. He began speaking precious promises to me about my marriage. He let me know He loved me. He said He understood why I was tempted and how much it hurt me to stay with Tracy, but right was still right and wrong was still wrong, and He wasn't going to change the rules for me.

And when He knew I was ready to hear it, He led me to Titus 2, which says older women are to teach younger women to love their husbands.

I was shocked. I didn't know this could be taught. I just figured either you did or you didn't. How unromantic would lessons in love be?

Besides, I thought I had a way out, and I told the Lord so. I didn't have an older woman to teach me. So there!

That's when He relayed the rest of the message: *He* would teach me.

Lesson number one? Do for Tracy what I wanted to do for this other man.

I knew God had to be kidding. But I realized He was completely serious. And I could start by cooking meals Tracy enjoyed.

I baked a cherry pie that didn't burn. And double peanut butter cookies. And a full roast dinner with mashed potatoes and gravy. And all his old favorites.

Then came other tasks I would have preferred doing for the other man. Wearing a dress I knew Tracy liked. Keeping my weight down. Having the house in order. Mowing the grass for him.

I started the projects amid many tears and much frustration. At one point, just the thought of acting loving toward Tracy made me physically nauseous. I wanted to scream in protest and quit the charade, but somehow God's grace enabled me to keep trying.

Eventually I realized that a truce had been reached. We were no longer arguing over every little comment or action. In a few weeks we even found a camaraderie we'd shared when we'd first met. I caught myself laughing at one of Tracy's corny jokes, and it wasn't just because I was playing a role; it was genuine appreciation for his sense of humor.

While I was working on doing loving things for Tracy, he was experiencing something new to our relationship: freedom. I had no expectations of him, and that released him to start tentatively showing me the love he had for me in his heart. He had quit doing that much earlier because I had rejected his displays of affection. But now he found new courage, and his shy attempts at expressing love were finding a home in my own heart.

I was the most surprised person of all when I found one day that my feelings for Tracy had blossomed into romantic love! God had instructed me to do loving things for Tracy—that's what he needed to communicate love to him. And Tracy's response to feeling loved also drew me in. Not only through his affirming words and loving touches, but the way he decided to stay with me, showing an unconditional love that transcended the love of a man and gave me a glimpse of God's heart for me.

Spending more time *showing* love than *looking* for it satisfied me with a fullness the finest kitchen couldn't provide. I never would have guessed that the way to Tracy's heart really *was* through his stomach! And that it was also the way to *my* heart, as I finally let him show me the love he'd carried for me all along.

Since those days, we've shared many happy meals in our kitchen. We added to those first three children—four adopted children and a surprise blessing of one last baby on the tail end. So far our eight children have given us sixteen grandchildren to love and feed— sixteen and counting, that is!

Our best talks are still at the kitchen counter, where we continue to discover what it means to put our love into action. The kids beg for our favorite recipes that speak love to them louder than words. And when my grandchildren perch on a stool with flour on one cheek and melted chocolate chips around their mouths as we mix a batch of cookies, I can only smile with gratitude to God. He has given us a heritage of love that I nearly threw away as easily as Esau gave up his birthright for a bowl of soup.

If I'd given in fully to temptation, I'd have missed the love of my precious husband and the subsequent opportunities God has given us to let that love overflow to others. God's cooked up a recipe for love sure to satisfy any appetite. Ahh, superb!

—BECKY YATES SPENCER

⌒

*F*eelings can be so elusive. And so often they lead us down the wrong paths. As Becky determined, what's right is right—no matter how she felt about it. And the same is true in our lives and marriages, even if we're not battling temptation to leave our love. We all have moments *when the grass seems greener in another pasture, and when we're over-come with the feeling that if we stay where we are, we'll starve.*

But the right thing to do is to continue to act upon fact, not emo-tions. To continue to act loving and kind even if we don't feel like it. There must be fifty ways to love instead of leaving! As we find those ways to show love, a surprising upheaval begins to happen in our lives. We start to feel the way we're acting!

It Began in the Nursery

We met in the nursery at church when I was just a bed baby. Almost a year older, she was crawling around on the floor. I don't remember a time when she wasn't part of my life. I have teased her and said it must have been the way she was wearing that diaper!

She was my date to the sweetheart banquet at church when we were in the fourth grade. She asked me to be her date following dancing lessons in the fifth grade. We did not date again until our senior year in high school.

Our first year in college was a challenge. I went north, she went south, and my phone bill went through the roof. The following summer I suggested that we both transfer to another college for our sophomore year. We did and our romance continued to bloom. Then, on my knee the old-fashioned way, I proposed marriage on her front porch at 303 Coffee Street in Talladega, Alabama.

When I was nineteen, we were married at the First Baptist Church in Talladega. In my new Mustang, we drove to Chattanooga for our honeymoon.

Realizing a married man needs to be gainfully employed, I found work as a nighttime DJ at a local radio station. She got a job working the cash register in a clothing store. The plan was for both of us to work at night and go to school during the day. She considered her job as a means to help support us. To me it was much different. I fell in love with my work.

Three years later I had moved several steps up the ladder and, at the age of twenty-three, was the manager of a new FM radio station. I had immersed myself in an exciting new career. Meanwhile, she was spending nights at home alone and pregnant, while her young husband was out entertaining clients and doing play-by-play sports.

Oblivious to the reality she faced, I chased success. While she taught at the Alabama School for the Deaf during the day, she also became virtually a single parent of three children over the next few years. I'm sure at some point she had to ask herself, "Is he worth it?"

In this temporary condition we call life, challenges come along that can be described as turning points. Mine came when our three-year-old daughter was diagnosed with leukemia. Suddenly the exciting career was no longer the most important thing in my life. Without the patience, faith, and love of my young wife, I don't know that I would have made it through those days.

The counselors at the hospital told us a crisis like this would usually either cause a marriage to fail or make it stronger. Judy's love, strength, and determination saw to it that ours was made stronger.

We were facing each other across our daughter's hospital bed, and I was crying; crying from a deep sense of hopelessness that comes only when your child is in danger and you know you can't do anything to help her her. In a soft yet firm voice, my wife said, "Only God loves this child more than we do, and I'm convinced

His will includes whatever is best for her. Matters of life and death are in His hands; our responsibility is to be her parents and prepare her for life while she's here."

Thankfully, our daughter survived childhood leukemia. For years she was part of a study of the long-term effects of chemotherapy on young children. She later went to college on a scholarship.

My daughter's illness had a positive effect on me. It didn't happen overnight, but it started there—right by our daughter's hospital bed—when I realized my career was not my most important responsibility in this world. My family was. Since that day I've paid more attention to my wife and have learned valuable lessons from her, including the true meaning of love.

While I haven't yet earned my master's degree in love and relationships, I'm becoming a better student. We spend more time together now, we enjoy one another's company more, and it's all because she was patient enough to stand by me when I was not standing by her. She has invested the time and emotional energy it took to lead me to the understanding I did not have as a young man.

Today she will tell you we are friends, that we enjoy life and have fun together. Fun is just a little spark, but it is the spark that lights the fuel of enthusiasm. A marriage, or any other important relationship for that matter, cannot be sustained beyond the point where enthusiasm wanes and the spark goes out.

As our fortieth wedding anniversary approached, one of my friends suggested that our marriage had lasted because my wife and I have always been in love with the same man.

Wanting to make such an important anniversary special, I ordered her a very nice gift from the Bass Pro Shop—an attractive camouflage nightgown! This is the kind of thing a debutante has to put up with when she marries a hopeless redneck.

To celebrate our anniversary, I offered to take Judy on a vacation to the beach or to the mountains. I even suggested New York or Paris—anywhere in the world to express my appreciation for her putting up with me for forty years. She said, "I'll think about it and let you know."

The night before the big day, she asked, "Do you have gas in your pickup truck?" (You can't be a redneck without a pickup truck.) We packed a picnic lunch and spent the day riding all the back roads in the county. We talked about the trail we had been down together with its rocky ridges and soft meadows, and we talked about the journey yet to come—adventures we have yet to enjoy together.

After laughing a bunch and crying some, we capped off the day by going skinny-dipping in Talladega Creek! Looking back, I'm glad we didn't go to Paris. It would have cost a lot more and would not have been half as much fun.

—BRYAN TOWNSEND

What are you most enthusiastic about in your life? It took illness for Bryan to learn he valued family more than anything else, even the career he loved. The Bible tells us that where our treasure is, that's where our heart will be. That's also where our enthusiasm will be.

In today's society, marriage is often seen as a joke. It's something to be laughed at, yawned at, or even scorned as too binding—not something to be passionate about. What would happen if we were more enthusiastic about our union? What would happen if we frequently made it clear that we love being married? How would that affect our own attitude? How would it affect our beloved's attitude toward us? What would it teach our children? And how would it impact others around us?

Think about it. Is your enthusiasm where your heart is?

From Soap Opera
to Fairy Tale

Love has a way of pulling you through the most difficult circumstances, even when the odds are against you. I discovered shortly after my second marriage just how strong the bond of love can be when my life suddenly seemed to cave in around me. Intertwining two families with teenagers and attempting to mesh them into one can be grueling and painful.

Anger, lies, cocky attitudes, and jealousy raged between our teens, but even that didn't prepare me for what was lying ahead. I never dreamed my life would turn out to be such a chaotic soap opera.

The saga began when I married Stephen. I was determined that my new home would be filled with peace, happiness, joy, and love. After escaping twenty-one years in an abusive marriage, I was even more determined to make this marriage work. I prayed life would finally settle down for me and that our children would find the stability they needed. My deepest desire was for us to be one big, happy family and live happily ever after.

However, my fairy-tale dream quickly transformed into one huge dysfunctional nightmare. Even though Stephen and I attended church regularly and held Bible studies in our home, that didn't stop Stephen's sixteen-year-old son, Timothy, from being arrested for armed bank robbery; my unwed eighteen-year-old daughter, Trish, from becoming pregnant; and my sixteen-year-old son, Daniel, from developing an addiction to pornography. My dream of a peaceful, fun-loving home quickly disintegrated into an angry den of lies, deceit, and turmoil.

Trish discovered she was pregnant within weeks of our marriage. Stephen became snide and unforgiving of her behavior. I was mortified to know he could be so harsh and judgmental. He felt that since she was single and pregnant, she was living an unacceptable lifestyle and would only be a burden to our new marriage. So he told her she wasn't welcome in our home.

I knew my daughter was a loving, warm, and compassionate young lady who was struggling through her own hurts and disappointments since my divorce from her daddy.

My heart ripped inside me as I watched Trish go live with a girlfriend. I didn't condone what she had done, but I loved my daughter and would never turn her away just because she made a mistake. With my marriage being so new and my insecurities from my previous marriage still hanging on, I wondered if I was supposed to choose between loves—my husband or my daughter.

I cried so hard from my brokenness that it was difficult for me to breathe. Stephen stood firm in his opinion and offered no compassion for my pain.

Now Timothy, on the other hand, was the apple of Stephen's eye. He could do no wrong. It didn't take long for me to learn that Timothy was number one in Stephen's life and no one would come between them. This unexpected turnaround in Stephen's attitude took me by total surprise. While we were dating he made me feel I was his one and only, which is how he won my heart. But now I was bewildered by the displacement of Stephen's love. I became wary of overstepping my boundaries as Timothy's stepmother.

Regardless of my warnings about Timothy's undesirable friends and outside influences, Stephen couldn't see anything but perfection in his son. Timothy was easy to love and was very convincing, but I wasn't blinded to the lies about his drug problem or his affiliation with gangs. When we received the telephone call that Timothy had been arrested for armed bank robbery, Stephen was appalled and shocked; appalled that the authorities would accuse his son of such a crime, and shocked to discover he was actually guilty. Disappointment and grief caused him to withdraw from everyone, including me.

Everything in Stephen's life came to a screeching halt. All meaningful communication between us ended, except for our prayer time together. Generally, I did all the praying while Stephen fell asleep, only to awaken when I said, "Amen." I had to watch the wording of my prayers for Timothy or we would end up in an argument, which would give him even more reason to distance himself from me.

The only time Stephen showed any excitement for the next several months was when we visited Timothy in prison. During those two-hour trips to the prison I would try to converse, but Stephen rarely responded. However, the instant he saw Timothy, his eyes sparkled, a smile broke across his face, and the two of them would talk nonstop through the entire visit. I felt out of place and unwanted.

Seeing Stephen's love for Timothy made jealousy rage within me. I yearned for Stephen to express his love for me in a similar way, but his silence shut me out. Every time I tried to console him, he pushed me away. I knew he was hurting for Timothy, but he couldn't see that I was hurting for him.

Since Stephen had distanced himself from me, my jealousy turned into anger toward him for his relentless judgment and rejection of Trish, when his own son robbed a bank with a loaded gun. Stephen put Trish out of the house but wanted to bring Timothy back home.

I hated the anger and unsettling feelings I was having about our marriage, so with no other recourse, I turned to my Bible for answers.

Questions bombarded my mind. *Do I really love Stephen? Certainly! Did I make a mistake? Absolutely not! Then why am I so unhappy? Because I don't feel loved! Why is all this bad stuff happening to us and to our kids? I don't know.*

As I pondered these questions in my mind, I began to realize that Stephen had some lingering turmoil from his previous marriage. He had been deeply hurt by his first wife's unfaithfulness. Her behavior caused him to have trust issues, which spilled over into our marriage. I felt so foolish when I finally realized that he didn't trust me with his pain. I needed to prove to him I could be trusted, but I didn't know where to start.

I immediately begged God's forgiveness for my jealousy, anger, and lack of forgiveness. I began to ask God to grant me wisdom and direction in dealing with our marriage and our kids. I didn't want to settle for a mediocre marriage. I wanted a strong marriage filled with compassion, love, and trust. Even though at the time I felt Stephen and I were strangers living under the same roof, I was determined more than ever to show my love for Stephen by giving him the time and space he needed to recover from Timothy's arrest.

Then, just as I thought I had a new handle on things, I found a porn movie in our DVD player. Daniel knew this type of material was prohibited in our home. Disappointment filled me and my face burned with anger as I pounded the DVD to pieces on the kitchen counter.

To my surprise, hidden in Daniel's room I found numerous porn movies, porn magazines, business cards from topless bars, pictures of night-club girls scantily dressed with their telephone numbers written on the back, plus all sorts of other sexual items. I was stunned. Obviously his addiction had been going on for quite a while, and I had been clueless.

I was livid and hurt—again! I was afraid to tell Stephen about my findings in Daniel's room. I wasn't sure he could handle another disappointment, and yet I wondered where earning Stephen's trust fit into this situation. If I were to tell him, he would explode, and I couldn't handle another outburst. I opted to remain silent.

My silence opened the door for depression to haunt me. Stephen and I were hurting, but in different ways. Since we hadn't had a real conversation in months, he had no idea there was another crisis in our home. We were drowning in painful disappointment in our children but couldn't find that common ground to open the communication gap between us.

I began to doubt the security of our marriage. I've always been non-confrontational, so all this drama in my life played havoc with my emotions. I searched my Bible for comforting Scriptures to help me hang on to *hope*, but I had difficulties knowing how to apply them to my heart. Even in my doubt, I continued to pray for my marriage and my family.

I knew Stephen was praying, too, but I didn't know if he included me in his prayers. This soap opera life wasn't what I bargained for at all, but I had purposed in my heart to love regardless of my own pain. I knew I had to make the difficult choice to forgive everyone, including myself.

Not only did I have to make the choice to forgive, but I also had to force myself to climb out of the quagmire of depression I was drowning in. I began to realize that I was returning to that self-preservation mode I had established during my first marriage.

I know God always hears our prayers, but one night in particular He had a special plan. As Stephen and I prayed together, Stephen actually stayed awake and prayed. God opened the door for us to begin talking to each other in a way that we hadn't talked in months.

It was a little disconcerting at first, but we managed to stick with it and not argue. We talked about all the attacks that had come against us and our marriage. Stephen began talking about his disappointment in Timothy, and I talked about my disappointment in his attitude toward my children and me.

After we discussed our feelings, we realized we acted independently, leaving each other out. Stephen and I apologized for our mistakes, expressed our love for each other, and promised to seek God's direction in all things from this day forward.

As we kept seeking God's direction in our marriage, we began to gradually see changes in the way we communicated, in our attitudes, and in our family situations. It didn't happen overnight, but with prayer and a conscious effort, we began seeing our marriage as a team effort.

Stephen's attitude eventually changed so much that he let Trish come back home. We continued to visit Timothy in prison until his release, and then we brought him home. Daniel went through some tough times and we suffered quite a bit of heartache from his teenage choices. But again, we faithfully prayed and God delivered him.

Today Stephen and I trust each other immensely, are happier than we ever thought possible, and know without a doubt it was all because of God's love, mercy, and grace that we survived.

–LORETTA J. EIDSON

*O*vercoming the pain in relationships is hard. And when we hurt—especially after a negative response from the one we love—well, it's tougher to open ourselves up to more hurt.

But one of the reasons God draws us together in marriage is so we'll have someone to walk on the road with us. Someone who will bolster us up when we're weak—even when it means mutual bolstering and leaning on each other to walk. Perhaps you've seen fragile elderly couples who lean together and balance each other as they walk, to help each other keep from falling.

Emotionally, we all should be like that. Yes, it's difficult to trust each other with our hearts when we've faced pain in our lives. And it's especially tough when we've been hurt by the one who is closest to us. But as we lean on each other, we make it through.

The Hurricane That Saved My Marriage

M y ten-year-old made a confession the other day.

"Mom," he said. "I know Hurricane Katrina was a bad thing, but I've never had so much fun with my family before."

He's right. Romans 8:28 promises, "God causes everything to work together for the good of those who love God and are called according to his purpose for them." That's certainly been the case for my family since Hurricane Katrina slammed our house an hour north of New Orleans. One positive result was relaxed time together as a family, courtesy of a month without electricity. Evenings that would have seen my husband, David, watching TV, me fiddling on the computer, and the kids doing various solo activities, had us huddled together by candlelight, talking and laughing.

Since the day we watched Katrina and subsequent tornadoes

devastate our rural community, God has opened our eyes to see new blessings every day, not the least of which has been a complete metamorphosis within my marriage.

Something happens when we're in fear for our lives that reduces even the most sophisticated of us to a primal state. When life hangs in the balance the way ours did the nine hours we rode out Katrina, all of our intellect, all of our reasoning, all of our worldly wisdom is stripped away—leaving only the bare, naked truth.

I guess that's what's meant by "being broken by God." I think I required more breaking than most people. From the day I gave my life to Christ, my biggest challenge has been letting go of the ideas of female independence etched on my brain. As many times as I read and reread Scripture verses about godly women and wives, such as in Ephesians 5, Colossians 3, and even in Proverbs 31:10–31, and as much as I knew that's what God was calling me to, those worldly messages seemed impossible to shake.

My mouth is my biggest enemy. I want to let David be the leader of our family. But when he doesn't lead the way I think he should, my mouth flies open and I find myself asking God to forgive me for disrespectful words to my husband *again*!

Then on August 29, 2005, there we were: huddled with our four kids in a hallway listening to windows exploding, the roof tearing away, and massive trees crashing within inches of the house. In an instant, submitting to my husband became the most natural thing on earth. I've never been so relieved not to be in charge as I was that day.

We found out later that our town had been hit by dozens of tornadoes spinning off of the hurricane. The devastation stretched for miles. It took us two days working with chain saws, handsaws, and axes just to cut our way to the outside world. Then we had to decide where we'd live, if we'd put the kids in school temporarily out of state, and whether David should accept a transfer, which would mean living apart for a while.

I'm sure the kids were stunned to hear me say things like,

"Whatever Dad says goes" and "We'll do whatever Daddy decides" rather than arguing my point of view.

But just as God opened our eyes the day of the storm to see that our house and all the things in it are just that—things that can be replaced—He opened my eyes in the days afterward to see the gift He's given me in a stable, intelligent, godly husband fully capable of leading his family.

As we spent days trying to track down family and friends and I found out my teaching position had been "discontinued," I felt an unexplainable peace knowing I was in God's will where my marriage is concerned. In the months since the hurricane, I've felt God's presence stronger than ever before. That presence assures me that He'll bring us through this, and when He does we'll emerge and grow closer to the image of Christ He intends for us.

I hate to admit that it took such a catastrophe for me to surrender to God's plan for my marriage, and I don't claim to have arrived yet. But God's mercy is new every morning. With His help we'll rebuild our lives, and through it all with God's grace I'll be the godly wife He wants me to be, one day at a time.

–MIMI KNIGHT

⌒

While marriage is a partnership, in every good partnership one person needs to take on the final responsibility. As Mimi found, accepting the role of partner instead of having to take ultimate responsibility all the time can be a blessing and relieve a lot of emotional stress!

The Bible indicates that in most marriages, the man is better suited to that role—after all, God did design men and women to be different not only physically but emotionally, too.

Not that following someone else's leadership is a piece of cake. It can be tough to trust another person, to step back and say, "Let's follow your plan of action," and then to adhere to our words with our behavior. It's tough to trust instead of criticizing.

And of course there's a flip side to this topic, too. Leadership is never to be used as a weapon. Where the Bible gives women the advice to submit to, or willingly follow, their husband's leadership in Colossians 3:18, the following verse instructs husbands to love their wives. When we love someone, we're going to listen to that person and try to please him or her and encourage and build up the person. Ephesians 5 takes it a step further and tells husbands to treat their wives as Christ treated the church, giving His life for it. And Ephesians 5 also tells believers to submit to each other.

Each married couple has to figure out how leadership plays out in a godly manner in their own marriage. Learning to trust a spouse not only builds confidence and often relieves some stress, but it also helps us learn to trust our ultimate leader: God.

$\mathcal{L}$ove in a Laundry Basket

The nurses wheeled my gurney back into the hospital room, tubes literally coming out of every possible place in my body. Still under heavy sedation from over five hours of surgery, I looked like "death warmed over," I was told.

As the nurses hooked me back up to my room monitors, John, my husband of four months, gently took my hand. He slid my still-glittering wedding ring back on my finger and whispered, "Will you marry me again?"

At that moment, as I slept through morphine, my lessons in real love began. They'd been hinted at a couple of months earlier when, barely back from our honeymoon, my husband learned that his father had died. Instantly, we were plunged out of newlywed bliss into the bitter reality of personal grief and family tragedy. Happiness turned to heartbreak as I sought to help my husband through a pain I couldn't fully understand.

But two months later, as we were still reeling from the emotional and financial impact of the sudden loss, we realized something was seriously wrong with me physically. Excruciating stomach pain clamped my insides like a vise grip. I couldn't keep food or liquid down. I weighed eighty-five pounds.

"I'm admitting you to the hospital now," the doctor said. "Your only choice in the matter is which hospital it will be."

Doctors, perplexed and concerned, searched for answers. John remained at my bedside for four weeks. He stayed through the tests, the long surgery, and the recovery. He arranged to work from my hospital room and slept in the chair next to me at night. The nurses called us "The Newlyweds."

Finally I was diagnosed with Crohn's disease, and part of my digestive tract was removed. When I was released from the hospital, the six-week recovery was difficult. John patiently cared for me as I regained strength.

Wearing an ostomy bag hardly makes a young bride feel sexy. I wrapped cloth around my waist to hide it, but it still distressed me. Although John said he saw me as beautiful, I felt far from attractive— hardly the bright, alluring bride my new husband deserved. Besides, he had enough to deal with in grieving for his father.

Instead of enjoying the honeymoon phase of marriage, we were thrown right into a mess. We were being asked to deal with things most couples don't deal with until they've been together for years. I quickly learned to help my husband through grief. He received a crash course in caretaking.

In my deepest parts, I wondered if we had the marital maturity to handle these issues without permanently wounding our fledgling relationship. I knew God had brought us together, but didn't He realize this could tear us apart? Too much pain. Too much grief.

So I donned an upbeat, positive face as much as possible. Oh, there were tears and times of crying out to God. But I decided I simply couldn't burden my husband with all the emotional and physical ugliness. I couldn't ask that of him. It might be too much.

I returned to the hospital three months later for surgery to reconstruct my internal systems. Again, John stayed by my side. After three more weeks, I came home to a similar recovery. But this time, I also faced a body trying to work normally again.

Let's just say my laundry wasn't always very pleasant. Surprisingly, a person's digestive system doesn't instantly remember what it's supposed to do and what warnings it should give. I again cried out to God and tried not to burden my husband with more than necessary.

John handled the cooking and cleaning as I got better. But I told him he should leave the messier portions of my laundry to me. I needed to strengthen myself with bits of light work, anyway.

I already felt unattractive, and this was incredibly humbling, even humiliating. I was supposed to be the blushing bride for other reasons. And now I worried that John might feel he'd been given a bad deal. This wasn't what he signed up for.

Then one day I saw John lugging clean clothes into our bedroom. I noticed that he had done my disgusting laundry. Deeply embarrassed at what he'd probably dealt with, I swallowed hard.

"You weren't supposed to do that!" I scolded.

He turned to me and softly said, "I'm your husband, and I love you. So what's the big deal? Let me take care of you. It's what I'm here for."

At that moment, my eyes watered as it dawned on me: *This* is love. *Real* love. John had taken the most humiliating part of my life and showed tender, compassionate care. He wouldn't leave me to face it alone. He would get right in the mess with me.

Flowers, gifts, romantic evenings. They're wonderful. But they are just the icing on the wedding cake. Right then, holding the laundry basket in his hands, John shouted, "I love you" more loudly than red roses ever could. Being in the ugliness and the pain of life together and seeing each other through, *that's* when we really speak our love. Ever since, I've challenged myself to find ways to quietly shout the same message of unconditional acceptance and service to him. Eight years later, I'm still striving to do so.

Don't get me wrong. John isn't perfect, and neither am I. We struggle like everyone else. But I think I learned something important as a wife. Facing the harsh sides of our wedding vows—for worse, for sicker, for poorer, and even (indirectly) until death—within six months of marriage taught me to find real romance in something deeper than candlelight and flowers. Often real love reveals itself in small, unheralded actions—dishes washed, a gas tank filled, or a tear shared.

Sometimes real love doesn't come wrapped in floral tissue or shiny paper. Sometimes it comes loaded in a laundry basket.

—DIANE GARDNER

Each of us has our shameful secrets, our humiliating moments, and our experiences so embarrassing that we don't even want our spouses to know about them. But as Diane discovered, sometimes we sell the one we love short. When we try to hide our messiness from a loved one, we're denying him or her the opportunity to help us and express love in the most profound way possible.

It's also a bit scary letting someone, even the one who's promised to love us for life, into those messy moments. We have to be brave enough to overcome our fear that the other person will reject us if we're not all poised and polished—whether it be physically, emotionally, or spiritually.

Dare to let yourself be loved. Dare to let the one who loves you most into the most intimate parts of your life, even if they're messy. That's where love flourishes and grows.

Engine Failure

I pause in the process of tucking my husband in. Tucking him in? Is that what I'm really doing?

It feels more like a bedtime ritual for one of my children when they were small. Get the pajamas on, adjust the pillow, say the prayers, settle the blanket, and give a kiss good-night. But to this routine I've added anxiety medication—and my presence until he falls asleep.

I sit holding his hand until he dozes off, wondering how we got here. When we married twenty-two years ago, I never thought my strong, laughing, dependable husband would beg me to stay awake with him all night because his mind was racing. I didn't foresee taking on all the parenting, bill paying, and *life* for the foreseeable future. I didn't expect my social husband to cry at the dinner table and choose sleep over company.

Depression is an enormous burden for the one who suffers. Even more when it's combined with anxiety. It's like walking through a long tunnel feeling as though there's no hope for a light to appear in the distance.

But for the spouse, it's a different kind of struggle. The depression colors all the relationships and activities that are a normal part of life. Though not saddled with the depression itself, the burden of carrying all the other responsibilities alone can leave you with little physical, mental, and emotional resources to help your partner walk through this difficult valley.

I remember attending an excellent seminar given by a long-time missionary named Cash Godbold. He had experienced major depression, and he likened the effect on his marriage to an airplane. He said that his despair made his marriage seem like a twin-engine plane in which one of the motors has failed. The plane was in serious danger of crashing. His wife—the other engine—had to put forth more than double the effort in order to keep their plane in the air.

As I think about our situation, I have definitely felt like that lone engine. It's not just the extra jobs and the worry. Words can hurt me deeply, and in my husband's anxious state he is unnaturally critical, which is heartbreaking for me when I'm trying so hard to keep all the balls in the air. Our comfortable marriage roles have been subjected to the blender, and I find myself at a loss for working on intimacy when I have the role of caregiver thrust upon me. It's no wonder that in marriages with a depressed spouse, the couple is much more likely to divorce. I'm desperate to keep my marriage from joining that statistic.

So I choose what many of us do when we're at the end of our rope. I throw myself at my Savior's feet, diving deep into His Word, allowing it to flow over me. I lift each tense moment to Him—the loneliness, anger, and resentment that my husband is unable to care for me emotionally. I also cast my worries before the Lord: the fear that he won't be able to keep his job, that I'll fall apart when he needs me most, and most of all that this will be the way things are forever.

I cry in the shower so I won't worry him. I sit in the car and pray over him before he heads to work and acknowledge that I'll probably have to meet him for lunch, just so he can make it through the day. As hard as it is for me to juggle my increased roles, I try to imagine myself in my husband's shoes—anxious and unsure if things will ever get better.

One of my greatest blessings is being a part of a four-woman prayer group that has met consistently for over nine years. These friends listen, encourage, support, and pray for me. They are my lifelines.

They help me step back and see the big picture—that besides taking care of everyone else, I need to take care of myself. It's essential for me to make time to do some things I enjoy, to remember to laugh and stop being so serious.

My friends encourage me to journal my struggles so I'll see God's hand in all this when the season is past. The Israelites set up altars whenever God did something amazing. Years later, when they passed by the altars with their children or grandchildren, the little ones would ask, "What are these rocks here for?" And the story would be told again, spreading to the next generation.

I'm determined to erect an altar of words that I can point my children to and say, "Remember the time when Daddy was so sick? When he asked you to pray for him at the dinner table because he was so anxious he thought he couldn't get through the meal? Do you recall how God cradled us in His hands, met our needs, and kept us going?"

And as I think about what I'll share with my children one day, I realize that God has answered in so many ways already. Somehow, I believe the pain of this trial should be so much greater than it actually is. It brings to my mind the cushioned bumper we bought for our coffee table when the kids were toddlers. If they fell and bumped their heads on the table edge, they still cried. It hurt. But not nearly as much as if that edge had been unprotected. I'm certain that God has softened the hardest edges of this experience for us all. And one of the sources of that precious gift is the prayers of our friends and family.

—DEBBIE MAXWELL ALLEN

Just as life isn't always fair, marriage isn't always fair. The tasks aren't always divided down the middle and the burdens aren't always shouldered equally. Sometimes one spouse will bear the brunt of caring for the home, bringing in the income, keeping the relationship going, and myriad other details. Sometimes one spouse has to keep going and shoulder most, if not all, of the responsibilities while the other one checks out for a time.

Being the partner who shoulders the relational, financial, or emotional burdens can be unbelievably frustrating and wearing. And sometimes when we're left in that position we can do nothing about it— except to pray and keep loving.

When we think we are at the end of our resources, an amazing occurrence happens—God steps in. He can fill the gap for us as we call on Him. When we reach the end of our resources, He can fill our reservoir. And when we are weary and heavy-laden, as He's promised in Matthew 11:28, He will bring us rest.

$\mathcal{A}$ Love That's Never Out of Fashion

Walking through the Salem Center Mall looking for a formal dress for my wife felt like trying to get on the right car of an Italian train—the clothing terms seemed like a foreign language to me, and the few words I did understand, like "Clearance" and "70 percent off," didn't exactly put me on the right track.

Linda and I had been married eighteen months when an older couple told me that buying something like a formal would surprise the socks off her. Since the senior banquet at the college where we worked was that night and Linda had already settled on wearing the same dress she'd worn the previous year, I knew she wouldn't be expecting a new one. So their idea to surprise her in this way sounded good to my young-husband ears.

"Can I help you?" I should have noticed the smirk on the

young sales associate's face as she practically blindsided me at the 70-percent-off rack. I lifted what I thought was the perfect dress from the rack and showed it to her.

Since I had only shopped with Linda for Christmas gifts, I really had no idea what styles she liked. So I went with what I liked—seemed logical enough since she wouldn't be able to see herself in the dress anyway.

"That's a pretty dress and it's a great price. You won't find a better bargain in the whole mall," the clerk purred, apparently sensing a commission. Her sales pitch sounded great, since I had no intention of shopping the "whole mall" anyway.

"You'll probably want a few accessories," she continued.

Thirteen minutes later I was back at our apartment.

I hung the dress on the front of the closet door. "This'll be the first thing she sees when she walks in. Will she be surprised!" I said to myself with satisfaction.

I should explain that Linda and I have different styles. I tend to be a little bit country, and she's a little bit rock 'n' roll. So you can probably guess what the dress looked like. Yes, it was pink. Not the West Coast kind of pink the college girls occasionally wore at that time. This was the soft, pastel pink that little girls dressed up in for tea parties.

And the length? Well, let's just say it was the only formal at the banquet that brushed the floor with sweeping layers of crinoline and lace. To finish off its country, 70-percent-off charm, each sleeve puffed up from the shoulder like a transparent cloud, and a pink sash tied the back into a perfect and prominent bow.

And the accessories the sales associate so appreciatively endorsed? White lace gloves and a matching hat. I pinned the gloves to the sleeves and the hat to the top of the hanger—to complete the stunning visual impact of my purchase. I guess if you were to sum it up using an allusion, this was a *Gone With the Wind* kind of dress—and I should have understood that is where the dress belonged—gone in the wind somewhere.

An hour later, Linda arrived home and raced to the bedroom to get ready for the evening. She stood stunned.

Yes! Just the reaction I was hoping for, I thought as I watched her wonder at the depth of my sacrifice and love.

At the banquet I took pictures of her gliding down the spiral staircase and standing beside her girlfriends. The contrast was so striking, I thought of the passage from the Song of Songs, "Like a lily among thorns is my darling among the maidens" (2:2 NIV).

Later that evening as she hung the pink dress at the very back of the closet, I reminded her, "Honey, tomorrow's Sunday. You could wear the dress again."

She turned toward me and smiled strangely, like a mentor hoping a mentally challenged student can understand a simple lesson.

"Did you see anyone else in a dress like this tonight?" she asked gently. The rich auburn in her eyes pulled at the highlights in her matching hair.

"Well, of course not, that's why you were so uniquely beauti—"

Then it hit me.

She *didn't like* the dress. But for some reason she'd worn it the whole evening without a single complaint—the lace, the prominent bow, and the crinoline beautifully complemented by her constant smile.

My mind wandered through the evening's events. The smiles and gestures of the college girls as Linda walked by. The huddled faculty wives looking her way. I had assumed they were stares of admiration, but Linda knew she'd been the topic of conversation for other reasons.

"Well, why didn't you say something?" I sank to the hope chest that crowded the foot of our bed. My Herculean quest had landed me facedown in the Augean stables.

She sat next to me and put her arms around my neck.

"Thanks for thinking about me," she whispered.

As she slept that evening, I stared at the black emptiness in the closet. Somewhere in there hung a dress—a frilly, old-fashioned thing—that would forever minister to me the simple freshness of her love.

That night, God added something special to the mall of my memories: a flesh-and-blood picture of what Jesus meant when He said that life is about more than food and clearance racks and clothes—that it's about His love pictured for us in the everyday sacrifices we make for each other. That's what I see each time I remember, each time I think about the dress that revealed her love.

—MARTY TRAMMELL

Hopefully your spouse won't be surprising you with clothes unless he or she has a fashion sense or knows what you like. But we all have those moments in life when a spouse tries to hit a home run and basically strikes out.

Most of us would have been tempted to gently set Marty straight from the moment of the unveiling. After all, Linda knew her dignity was at stake. She knew others would probably laugh. But she preferred to lose her dignity rather than watch her husband lose his. She realized how pleased and proud he was to surprise her.

Perhaps the next time we get a surprise that isn't as delightful as intended, we can remember the joy that goes into planning, take a look at our lover's face, and find the grace to enjoy the intention. Few things express our love so well!

$\mathcal{L}$earning to Swim

Y ou can do this. Just take a deep breath and fill your lungs with air."

I obeyed my husband, keeping my eyes locked on him and ignoring the splashing all around us in the pool.

"Now fall back on the water and let your feet rise to the top."

I spread my arms wide, sank back, and pushed myself off the pool's floor.

"You're doing it," he said. "You're floating!"

I floated for almost five seconds before I panicked. The sheer act of surrender was too much. I simply could not trust the water to hold me, so I started splashing with my feet and thrashing with my arms until I really did sink.

Allen pulled me up with one arm. He ignored my coughing and spitting and guided me to the shallow side of the pool. "I know you can swim," he said again. "You were doing great floating on your back until you panicked."

"Well, you're wrong," I said. "I took lessons every summer of my childhood and never got past Station Two. I was the only kid who sank in the jellyfish float. I cannot swim."

I don't think either of us understood how perfectly we were describing our marriage bed in that exchange. Allen was convinced I could swim there, too. I was pretty sure I would have to settle for dog paddling the rest of our lives while he enjoyed a jet ski. And I thought I was content.

We had two daughters by then, so I convinced myself things were working okay in that department. I underestimated, though, how much strain lived between us because of our differing expectations.

Allen and I met when I was a naïve high school senior and he was a college freshman with a lottery number of 42 in the last draft for Vietnam. Like many of our friends, we rushed into adulthood fearing our dreams might march off in uniform, never to be seen again.

Seven years later the passion that had drawn us turned into friction between us. I was always tired. Little people were pulling on my body all day long. Between our own daughters and the children in my home day-care business, someone was always hanging off one of my limbs. By 9 p.m. every night, I was ready for a little space. The last thing I wanted was someone else reaching for me.

One afternoon Allen came into the kitchen where I stood between two huge stacks of dirty laundry. The children were napping, and I was digging through the piles for the most urgent items to wash. Allen watched for a minute and then said, "I'm just wondering. When will one of my shirts come to the top of the pile?"

Once again we were talking without talking. I knew he was asking for something more than a clean shirt, but I pretended not to understand. I pulled a plaid shirt from the bottom of the pile and tossed it into the washer. "Happy?" I asked.

I'm sure he wasn't.

During the next few months Allen came to a firm conclusion. We were done having children. He felt our physical intimacy was suffering from my exhaustion, and our marriage was suffering from lack of intimacy. We could fix all that by calling our family complete and giving the girls a little time to grow. Since I'd gone into marriage hoping for ten children, two didn't seem like a fair compromise.

Instead of saying anything, though, I just gritted my teeth. And I made a point of staying on the beach as much as possible. When Allen did guilt me into taking a swim, I often found I enjoyed myself. Sometimes it was even quite stupendous. Yet I dreaded the thought of dipping my toes in each time. It seemed like so much work. We stopped talking about it, but our unhappiness came out in other ways. I fought depression and he worked double shifts.

A few months later Allen came home with a serious expression on his face. "We need to talk," he said. The girls were already asleep, and I'd been pretty close to it myself. But I managed to sit up and look focused. I braced myself for what might be coming next, but I was still unprepared.

"I think we are supposed to have another baby," he said. "And I think it is going to be a son."

He went on to explain how God had been dealing with his heart on the matter of fatherhood.

"And about our relationship," he said. "I want you to know I love you for you, not just your body. If I have to hold you all night long with no expectations of anything else just to prove that to you, I will."

Something changed in both of us that night. Suddenly our love had a new purpose. A purpose beyond ourselves, beyond our own pleasure, and beyond the passion of our youth. And that, of course, is the secret of great sex. It has to be about someone else.

In the next thirty days, I learned to swim. At first, our nightly rendezvous were about conceiving a baby. But pretty soon love-making became about pleasing the other person instead of just being pleased. I discovered the thrill of abandoning myself to the waves, of yielding myself—body, heart, and soul—to someone else. I managed to fall back into the water and stop fighting for my own footing.

Our son will be thirty years old this year, and these days his father and I live in a delightfully empty nest. We still love the water. We swim. We float. We ride the waves. And sometimes we go deep-sea diving in places so wonderful it takes our breath away.

I think the high dive is next.

—KATHY NICKERSON

*A*s Kathy says, *the secret to great sex is that it has to be about pleasing someone else. We can ultimately enjoy this great intimacy the best when it's not just about ourselves and our desires and our needs. The joy comes in learning what our lover's needs are and meeting those needs.*

And isn't that ultimately the secret to a great marriage, too? Jesus said, "There is no greater love than to lay down one's life for one's friends" (John 15:13).

That's what keeps the flames flickering in a love affair. Giving, sacrificing, laying aside our individual needs and desires. Such actions never go unnoticed. And seldom go unrequited.

Do you want not just a great sex life, but also a great marriage? Take the time to learn what your spouse needs and freely give it. You'll find a satisfaction beyond belief—and a marriage that's truly made in heaven.

ABOUT THE CONTRIBUTORS

Jeff Adams is a writer, teacher, inspirational speaker, and pastor. He lives in Arizona with his wife, Rosemary, and their daughter, Meaghan. Email jeffadams@frontiernet.net for information on speaking topics.

Debbie Maxwell Allen lives high in the Rocky Mountains—a far cry from her Brooklyn roots. Debbie homeschools four teenagers and encourages teen and mom writers. She blogs at *Writing-WhileTheRiceBoils.blogspot.com*.

Deena Andrews enjoys spending time writing while raising four daughters, homeschooling, and encouraging others. She lives near Kansas City with her husband and daughters.

C. Michael Bobbitt is director of Second Mile Ministries, helping urban kids and their families in Kansas City. He edits the ministry's newsletter, is author of *Jesus Teaches 30 Days of Faith*, and his play *The Trial* has been performed throughout the country.

Judy Bodmer is the author of numerous articles and two nonfiction books, *What's in the Bible for Mothers* (Bethany House) and *When Love Dies* (Thomas Nelson). She's also a writing mentor.

Dave Branon, formerly managing editor of *Sports Spectrum* magazine, is an editor for Discovery House Publishers. He has written for *Our Daily Bread* since 1988, and has written fifteen books, the latest being *Beyond the Valley,* devotionals designed to help people going through life's tough times.

Ginny Dent Brant is an educator, writer, speaker, and soloist from Seneca, South Carolina. She is married and has three sons. Her book *Finding True Freedom: From the White House to the World* will be released in 2011.

Tonya Brown is a freelance writer and photographer, public speaker, educator, and mentoring coordinator in Wilmington, North Carolina. Contact her at tonya_j_brown@msn.com.

Annettee Budzban enjoys writing, speaking, and coaching others to help them accomplish their life goals. Her Web site is *AnnetteeBudzban.com*, and you can reach her by email at AnnetteeBudzban@aol.com.

J. F. Bunger has been a stay-at-home mom and helpmate for fifteen years. She's now pursuing a biblical studies degree at Calvary Bible College.

Kitty Chappell, international speaker and award-winning author of two books, *I Can Forgive If I Want To* and *Good Mews, Inspurrrrational Stories for Cat Lovers,* lives in Chandler, Arizona. *www.kittychappell.com.*

Zeta Davidson and her husband celebrated forty-two years of marriage. Besides being a wife, she's instructed nearly 2,000

Marriage & Family students at the high school and college levels. Email: zetadavidson@earthlink.net.

Janet Perez Eckles lives in Florida with Gene, her husband of thirty-four years. She is a writer, international speaker, and author. *www.janetperezeckles.com*.

Loretta J. Eidson is the author of *Good Ole Spiritual Food*, has written several articles for *Faith Café* Teaching Curriculum, and has a story in Gary Chapman's book *Love Is a Verb*.

Marsha Fisher and her husband, Jeff, launched *www.porntopurity .com* to offer encouragement and resources to couples struggling with pornography. Marsha is a professional communicator and a graduate of Southwestern Baptist Theological Seminary.

Cheryl Freeman works in publishing and teaches writing for English as a Second Language part time at a community college. She is passionate about missions, reading, and enjoying God's creation.

Jeff Friend is an award-winning freelance writer and speaker who lives in Florida with his wife, Nancy. He can be contacted at wordsofafriend@msn.com.

Diane Gardner lives at the foot of the Rockies. She holds a BA in Journalism and an MA in Mass Communications. She runs a freelance editing business and enjoys reading, oil painting, and attending the theater.

Mary Potter Kenyon lives in Manchester, Iowa, with her husband, David, and four of their eight children. Her writing has been featured in several magazines and anthologies.

Mimi Knight is a freelance writer living in South Louisiana with her husband, David, four kids, and too many dogs. Visit her blog at *http://blog.nola.com/faith/mimi_greenwood_knight/*.

Kathleen Kohler and high-school sweetheart, Loren, celebrate thirty years of marriage. They live in the Pacific Northwest and have three children and seven grandchildren. Visit her at *www.kathleenkohler.com*.

Jan Lucas lives with her husband, Steve, in Airmont, New York. They have been married forty-eight years and have three sons. She is currently active as a Hospital Certified Harp Therapist.

Kevin Lucia is a full-time English teacher finishing a master's degree in Creative Writing at Binghamton University. His fiction, nonfiction, and poetry have been published in several journals and anthologies.

Harriet Michael was born in Africa, is the daughter of missionaries, and lives in Louisville, Kentucky, with her husband. She is a freelance writer, the mother of four, and the grandmother of one.

Kathy Collard Miller (*www.KathyCollardMiller.com*) is a popular women's conference speaker and the author of forty-nine books, including *Women of the Bible: The Smart Guide to the Bible* series (Thomas Nelson).

Wendy Miller's stories have been published in inspirational books and on numerous Web sites. She enjoys writing novels, spending time with family, and hiking. Feel free to visit her blog, *http://thoughtsthatmove.blogspot.com/*.

Dena Netherton is a freelance writer as well as musician and teacher. She has authored three novels, several children's plays, and children's songs. She lives in the Colorado Rockies with her husband.

Kathy Nickerson writes from northeast Missouri, where she also works in her husband's medical office, enjoys friendships with her children, and revels in her grandkids. Read more of Kathy's work at *www.kathynick.com*.

Emily Osburne is the author of *Everyday Experts on Marriage*. She and her husband, Clay, lead marriage workshops for young couples in the Atlanta area.

Connie K. Pombo is an author, speaker, freelance writer, and founder of Women's Mentoring Ministries in Mt. Joy, Pennsylvania. She can be reached at *www.conniepombo.com*.

Jim Rawdon is a pastor who retired on disability after an accident. Until forty he was a partner in a men's clothing business. He cares for Glenda in Lee's Summit, Missouri.

Kelli Regan is a writer and graphic designer who's learned firsthand there is *definitely* gain on the other side of pain. She's excited to see what adventures lay ahead in the next twenty years of marriage.

Lynne Rienstra writes mother/daughter Bible studies (*www.you growgirl.typepad.com*). She and her husband, Rob (a *hopeful* romantic), have been married twenty-eight years, have two children, and serve Trinity Presbyterian Church near Atlanta.

Dayle Allen Shockley is an award-winning writer whose by-line has appeared in dozens of publications. She is the author of three books and a contributor to many other works, including multiple *Chicken Soup* titles. Email her at dayle@ dayleshockley.com.

Pamela Sonnenmoser is a Christian speaker, writer, and personality trainer. She is on faculty with CLASSeminars. Pamela and her husband, John, live on their family farm near Kansas City, Missouri.

Becky Yates Spencer is a singer/songwriter, speaker, and author still cooking for Tracy in Kansas. Read more of her journey in *When Prince Charming Falls Off His Horse . . . and You've Become His Nag!*

Rhonda Wheeler Stock is a special-needs educator and lives with her husband and daughter—and near her sons and the cutest grandbaby in the world—in Lenexa, Kansas.

MaryEllen Stone, keynote speaker and author, has been published in numerous magazines and reviews. She is author of *Run in the Path of Peace—the Secret of Being Content No Matter What.*

Don Sultz, a freelance author and cartoonist, has been a full-time associate pastor for twenty-two years, specializing in children's ministries. He's the proud grandfather of four.

Bryan Townsend is a member of the Professional Speaker's Hall of Fame and was featured as one of the Hot 25 speakers in the industry by *Speaker Magazine* (August '09).

Marty Trammell is the English Chair at Corban College and is a Youth and Family pastor at Valley Baptist Church in Perrydale, Oregon. He and his wife, Linda, also enjoy reading, camping, fishing, and shopping—as long as Linda picks out the clothes!

Roberta Updegraff and her husband, Mark, remain sweethearts after thirty-six years. She travels throughout the world to write for Presbyterian Disaster Assistance Mission and is a substitute teacher in Williamsport, Pennsylvania—teaching everything from drama to auto mechanics to orchestra.

Brenda Wood is a motivational speaker who is known for her commonsense wisdom, sense of humor, and quirky comments. Her latest book is *Heartfelt: 366 Devotions for Common Sense Living.*

Be Inspired by What Love Can *Do*
From Bestselling Author
Gary Chapman

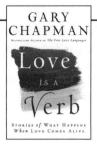

Dr. Gary Chapman, author of the *NY Times* best-seller *The Five Love Languages*, has seen love change lives. In *Love Is a Verb*, he shares these powerful stories and shows how you can apply the same principles in your own life. He also offers insight on a simple but profound concept—a concept that will help you become a more loving person, transforming your relationships with everyone from your spouse to your enemy.

"Love is not just a feeling. It's a choice. It's an action. Love is a verb." —Gary Chapman

Love Is a Verb by Gary Chapman